THE GOD OF HOPE

THE GOD OF HOPE

Finding True Hope in the
Midst of Life's Struggles

Annette J. Leroux

Copyright © 2018 by Annette J. Leroux

All rights reserved. No part of this publication may be reproduced, distributed, or transmitted in any form or by any means, including photocopying, recording, or other electronic or mechanical methods, without the prior written permission of the publisher, except in the case of brief quotations embodied in critical reviews and certain other noncommercial uses permitted by copyright law.

Published by Morning Dove Media.

All Scripture quotations, unless otherwise indicated, are taken from the Holy Bible, New International Version®, NIV®. Copyright ©1973, 1978, 1984, 2011 by Biblica, Inc.™ Used by permission of Zondervan. All rights reserved worldwide. www.zondervan.com The "NIV" and "New International Version" are trademarks registered in the United States Patent and Trademark Office by Biblica, Inc.™

Scripture quotations marked KJV are taken from the Holy Bible, King James Version.

Scripture quotations marked (NLT) are taken from the Holy Bible, New Living Translation, copyright ©1996, 2004, 2015 by Tyndale House Foundation. Used by permission of Tyndale House Publishers, Inc., Carol Stream, Illinois 60188. All rights reserved.

Cover photo: Sunrise in the Mountains, by Jean Beaufort on www.publicdomainpictures.net

Printed in the United States of America

"May the God of hope fill you with all joy and peace as you trust in Him, so that you may overflow with hope by the power of the Holy Spirit"

Romans 15:13

This book is dedicated to all those wounded souls who are beaten down, world weary and yearning for a better tomorrow.

There is reason for hope!

CONTENTS

1. The Search for Hope — 1
2. Hope for Protection — 21
3. Hope for Provision — 45
4. Hope for Healing — 73
5. Hope for Forgiveness — 101
6. Hope for the Lonely and Brokenhearted — 127
7. Faith - Hope's Cousin — 151
8. Doubt - Hope's Saboteur — 171
9. Hope Deferred — 187
10. Waiting on God — 207
11. Helping Yourself Find Hope — 235
12. Jesus, the Ultimate Source of Hope — 265

Sources — 285

Chapter 1

THE SEARCH FOR HOPE

Yes, my soul, find rest in God; my hope comes from Him.
Psalm 62:5

For I know the plans I have for you, declares the Lord, plans to prosper you and not to harm you, plans to give you hope and a future
Jeremiah 29: 11

HOPE. What comes to mind when you hear that word? You might be thinking that's a pretty loaded question, right, but what does the word hope mean to you? What would be on a list of the things you hope for on any given day? If you took a moment to think about more noble causes, your list might include world peace, or an end to poverty and all suffering in the world. As far as your own life is concerned, though, what do you hope for? What are those things which would keep your life on course and moving in a positive direction? Would some of the things on your list include healthy relationships with family and friends, or perhaps more of a focus on career and financial goals? Maybe your list would include smaller things that mean something special to only you. While hope may mean different things to different people, for all of us it's an important part of our daily existence. It's a powerful motivator behind a person's plans and dreams for the future. But what if you're at a point in your life where you have very little hope? You may have started your journey through life filled with positive expectations about the future, but over the years that hope has slowly disappeared. Were you once the proverbial "glass half-full person", but now have become the "glass almost empty" type? Does the thought of tomorrow fill you with excitement, or does it leave you worried and even on the edge of despair? Has the world and its' problems stolen the optimism about the future you once had? If so, do you ever wish that you could somehow recapture the enthusiasm for life that you're now missing? Do you think that's even possible, or are you afraid that hope is gone forever?

The world we live in promises to provide all that we need in terms of material security and success. Turn on the TV or radio during an election year and you'll be inundated with promises for the hope of a better life, if only you vote for this or that candidate. Despite the promises, each political cycle seems to bring more economic hardship, unrest and worries for the future than the one before. Advertisements promise happiness and fulfillment if we just buy a certain car, take this brand of antidepressant, or eat at that particular restaurant. Yet the world's promises for a more hopeful tomorrow inevitably fall short. How many times have you read about a person who won the lottery: an unimaginable sum of money that allowed that

The Search for Hope

individual to retire and live the easy life, only to then find that a few years later that "lucky" person is in worse shape than before picking those winning numbers… either divorced, broke, or even murdered, as was the fate for one poor winner. A few reading this might be saying, "Well, let me win that lottery, and I'll prove that I'm the exception!" The point I'm trying to make is that hope that relies on the promises of the world can be hollow and short lived. Does the search for real hope embody more than we can physically attain in this life? Can true hope be found in material success, or does it involve a deeper understanding of the spiritual aspects of life? And ultimately, if the world can't provide lasting hope for your life, where do you turn to find real hope?"

Right now, if you were to rate yourself on how hopeful you are about your future, where would you rank? On a scale of one to ten, with ten being the overflowing cup and one resembling the Sahara desert, where would you be? If your cup "runneth" on empty, what has happened in your life to get you to that point? Certainly life events influence our outlook on the world. Someone who has had a happy childhood, and has grown up knowing physical and emotional security, will probably find it easier to look favorably on the world than someone who has had to struggle through most of their life. Even a sheltered, trouble-free early life, however, does not guarantee a hopeful attitude forever. Life often has a way of evening the score with the passage of time. Loss of loved ones, relationship challenges, illness, and financial difficulties all temper our daily assessment of life. There are exceptions, of course. You can probably name individuals in your circle of family and friends who maintain an optimism that defies the series of bad circumstances that life may have thrown at them. Likewise, there are certainly folks who have a rotten attitude about everything, despite having all the conveniences and advantages of a privileged existence. What accounts for the difference?

Certainly, what life throws at you can temper even the most positive of attitudes. When you're getting hit with trial after trial, your natural resistance to despair can be worn down, especially when those trials never seem to end. I think one of the greatest enemies of hope, as least as it has been for me, is how long the difficulties in your life last. It's easier to maintain a more hopeful attitude when your problems have an end point. When your troubles seem to stretch on forever and there is no resolution in sight… that's when hope begins to fade. How does someone with Lou Gehrig's disease, who knows what the disease does to a person, see any bit of hope in his situation? For the recent widow who has been happily married for fifty years and cannot remember what life was like without her husband by her side…how does she muster the hope she needs to face each long and lonely day? The consolation that the world has to offer cannot ease the burden and uncertainty of the future that these individuals face. The world cannot provide the unfailing hope that any of us yearns for. So if the world cannot offer any sense

The Search for Hope

of real hope to a suffering soul, where can real hope be found? The answer lies in the truest source of hope, our eternal heavenly Father.

In our search for hope, the critical difference between the way the world looks at life versus the way God's children look at life is where each group sets its sight. It's only natural that while here on this earth, we focus on what we can see…the here and now, if you will. But we can get so bogged down trying to pay the bills, taking care of young children and elderly parents, handling health issues and the many other demands of work and home life, that we can't see the big picture. If we could gain the eternal perspective, and view our lives as a stepping stone to the true joy and hope that will follow this earthly life, our current troubles and challenges wouldn't seem so overwhelming.

When you rely on the world and its promises for your hope, you may reach some temporary satisfaction through your efforts. The successful pursuit of wealth can certainly seem to be an effective antidote to the problems you may be facing. Whatever problems can't be fixed or overcome by your own efforts can be forgotten or minimized with any number of earthly coping mechanisms. Substance abuse, unhealthy relationships and other unwise choices run rampant because people try to escape problems they're unable to face on their own.

You probably don't need me to tell you that life has more than its' fair share of problems. You may have learned firsthand about life's cruelties from tragedies and hardships you've experienced in the past or are currently experiencing. Maybe that's why you're holding this book in your hands right now. You may be feeling battered, bruised and exhausted from everything you've been facing. In fact, you may be wondering how your life turned into something you hardly recognize anymore. Certainly, this was not the life you had imagined for yourself so many years ago, when the future seemed to hold such promise. How did a life that was so full of expectant optimism become one of ever increasing despair?

Somewhere along the way, we as humans decided that our perception of fairness should govern the way the world works. If we do good, then good should be returned to us in like manner. That only seems fair, right? But what happens when things don't work the way we have decided they should work? What happens when your attempts at leading a good and righteous life are met with injustice and suffering? Can't it turn your world upside down? You may feel like you've done everything you were supposed to do. You've worked hard to get a good education yet now you're struggling to find a decent job. You've committed your life and considerable energy to being the best spouse you knew how to be, yet suddenly you find that the one who promised you "until death do you part", is having an affair. You've devoted a good portion of your life to raising God fearing children, but now those very children have turned their backs on God and you. You were doing your best to walk the

The Search for Hope

path you thought God had laid out for you in business, only to find that your other partners were playing by their own set of rules. Instead of the Golden Rule, they were thinking only of maximal profits and minimal ethics, which left the business on the edge of insolvency. You eat right and exercise, but still come home from the doctor with a grim medical diagnosis. Where is the fairness in any of these things? How do we maintain hope in the face of these types of setbacks?

One of the toughest things for us is accepting that life doesn't always work the way we want it to. No matter how hard we try, we can't bend events in life to our will. Circumstances occur without our permission and often without any warning. Because of this unfortunate reality, it's essential that we have something solid to hold on to when the ground starts shaking under our feet. Hope provides that solid foundation when all the other things we have been clinging to are stripped away.

Hope might be looked at as the life preserver in the storms of life. With hope, a person can keep trying despite facing tremendous obstacles. Without it, a person can give up when success may be just within reach. Have you ever been in a situation where you felt that hope was the key in whether you kept trying or decided to quit? As long as you clung to that hope, you could muster the strength needed to tough things out? How long you were able to cling to that hope made all the difference. When times are tough, and hope is vanishing, the dark storm clouds seem all the more threatening. But what if you could find

The God of Hope

a hope that could handle anything that the world threw at you? Would you be interested in a hope that wouldn't disappoint you no matter how bad your life got? It's my prayer that the words in this book will help you embark on a journey to find the true source of hope for your life. It's a hope that will exceed your greatest expectations, for it relies on a foundation that is ever present and never changing. It's the hope that is found in the author and originator of hope…in God the Father and His Son Jesus Christ. Real hope lies in the direction of the cross.

How would you respond if I told you that God looks at your life with nothing but hopeful expectation? What would you say if I told you that God's desire for you is to embrace and relish every moment of your life, and to find indescribable joy in each day that He has given you? That He wants you to thrive, not just survive, in the life that He has blessed you with? Would you be a little skeptical about that? Would your answer to me be that "If God wanted me to enjoy life, then why has He made it so difficult for me?" Of course, no one can know the mind of God and why He allows what He allows in our lives. I would suspect, however, that all our earthly experiences are orchestrated by the God who wishes to have a close personal relationship with us, intent on securing an eternal future for each and every one of us. Our response to Him can take one of two paths. We can choose to search for our own brand of hope, leaving God out of the process. Or we can acknowledge that life is too big and

The Search for Hope

burdensome for us to make it on our own. We are ready to admit that we need God and His hope.

If you're at a point in your life where you've finally realized it's better to grab hold of God's hope than to cling to your own version, then you're definitely headed in the right direction. But for some of us, that can still be hard to do. For Christians in particular, the questions associated with life's difficulties and God's promises can create a conflict of the heart and soul. Christians are supposed to believe wholeheartedly in the promises of God, right? But reading about those promises and knowing them in your head can often be easier than embracing those same truths in your heart. Practically applying those truths to daily life can become a steep uphill battle, especially in the midst of hard times. I know that I have experienced days where I wondered why God's Biblical promises didn't provide the measure of comfort that I thought they should. It was while reading my Bible one day that I came across a verse that really grabbed my attention. I'm sure that at some point in the past I had read this verse before, but on this particular day it seemed to jump off the page at me. The verse in question was Romans 15:13, and this is what it said…"May the God of hope fill you with all joy and peace as you trust in Him, so that you may overflow with hope by the power of the Holy Spirit". After reading it over several times, what struck me about it was the totality and depth of its optimism. It's a verse brimming with promise for the future.

The God of Hope

The first portion of this verse, of course, contains the title and pre-eminent message of this book. God is the "God of hope". I'll repeat that again because it's this truth that lays the bedrock foundation for the pages to follow. God is the God of hope! Not you or I, or anything else in this world. Nothing can provide the hope that God can in your life. As reassuring as that statement is, what's even more comforting is that God is described as being associated with hope. Not the God of vengeance, or the God of discipline, but the God of hope!

In your own life, how would you characterize God? How would you define your relationship with Him? Is He a loving God, or is He distant and aloof? Do you feel that you can run to Him with your problems and worries, like you would to a loving earthly father? Or do you mentally cower when you think of all your shortcomings and of what God must think of you? Can you picture God as the answer to life's problems, or do you feel that He has abandoned you and couldn't care less about any of your struggles? Here in this verse, however, is a God who above all is a loving Father who wants to provide a rich and hopeful life to you.

The belief that God is the true source of hope in this world is one that can be difficult to accept. We're assaulted daily with news events and philosophies that seek to deny the existence of God or of any hope that He might be capable of providing. So often we're conditioned to focus on how we can solve our own problems and provide our own measure of hope. It

The Search for Hope

can be hard to change our way of thinking… to accept that God wants to give us a sense of hope that the world is so incapable of giving.

I'll admit that when I think of God, I don't first think of Him as the source of hope. I can easily picture God as a stern disciplinarian. I can picture Him as a lawgiver. On fewer occasions I can picture Him as a loving Father. I have a hard time looking at God as someone who wants to give me a reason to be positive about the future. I'll be the first to admit that the problem lies with me and my view of the world as it is. Maybe it comes from hearing a few too many sermons on the Law instead of the Gospel. Whatever the reason, though, it takes a focused effort on my part to see God as the merciful God that He truly is. I suspect there are a few of you reading this who might feel the same way. But here is this verse in the Bible, the written word of God, where there's no uncertainty about this truth. There's no question here that God is the ultimate source of hope. He's the active donor and we are to be the willing recipients of this most precious gift. It isn't about us working to find or earn it, or anything remotely related to getting it through our own efforts. God is offering it to us for free!

If you search the internet for an explanation of hope, you'll find a number of slightly varying descriptions. Hope is described as a "confident expectation." According to answers.com, to hope is to "wish for something with expectation of fulfillment." Wikipedia defines hope as "the emotional state which promotes the belief in a positive outcome related to events and circumstances in one's life." These definitions may reflect different perspectives on hope, but what they have in common is that there exists an expectation for something good. When you hope, you're looking forward to a better day, perhaps the fulfillment of a particular dream, or perhaps rescue from whatever trials and challenges you may be facing in your life. Hope implies relief and a brighter future than the one you may be experiencing now.

So what does God, this supplier of hope, want to do for you? If you read on in Romans 15: 13, you'll find that He wants to provide you with all joy and peace. Do you have any joy or peace in your life right now? Do you even really know what it means to have either one in your life? Merriam Webster defines joy as the "emotion evoked by well-being, success or good fortune or by the prospect of possessing what one desires." While that definition certainly gives us the basic feeling for joy, it also tends to focus on the world's view. I've heard it said that there is a distinction between joy and its secular counterpart, happiness. Happiness is described as a feeling that's dependent on one's circumstances, while joy is described as being present irrespective of those circumstances. When things are going well in your life, you have happiness. When you lose your job, or illness strikes, that happiness often evaporates. Joy, on the other hand, is not limited by the good or bad things that are happening in your life right now. No matter the pain or suffering you may be experiencing, the joy which fills your soul is a stabilizing force that keeps the ship upright in the face of gale force winds. Joy is the bedrock of contentment, while happiness is that superficial layer of sand that gets washed away when the storms of life roll through.

Peace, as defined by Merriam Webster, is a "state of tranquility or quiet." Such tranquility can be hard to find in this troubled world of ours. There's no shortage of things to be concerned or worried about on any given day. Rarely do I run into someone who tells me how at peace they are in their life. I'm guilty of the same…I have no problem focusing on the daily anxieties and obstacles that I encounter at work, home or church. I often find that the days' troubles rob me of what little tranquility I can muster on my own. Can you imagine what it would be like to be filled to the brim with *both* joy and peace, and not have to do anything to get it but trust in God? In Philippians 4:6-7, God gives us an inkling of what He means. "Do not be anxious about anything, but in everything, by prayer and petition, with thanksgiving, present your requests to God. And the peace of God, which transcends all understanding, will guard your hearts and your minds in Christ Jesus". It sounds too good to be true, doesn't it? If I'm completely honest with myself, I can think of no day in my life where I wasn't anxious about something. Even if I'm having a great day, there's always something to be at least a little concerned about. Could you imagine what even a single day without <u>any</u> worries would be like? Your job would be to spend your time talking with God and thanking Him for the life He has given you, and He would take care of the rest. What's even more comforting is verse seven, where God speaks about that elusive peace "which transcends understanding". The type of peace that God can give you and me is not dependent on our external circumstances. In effect, there is no direct relationship between how well your life is going and how much peace you are experiencing. This can be a hard concept for some people to accept, because in this world, so much of our worldly peace depends on daily events in our lives. When things are going well, you can feel relatively peaceful, but how can you be at peace when the world is falling apart around you? The answer lies in the incredible power of God to bring that peace into your life. There have been very few times in my life where I have felt that kind of peace: when there was no earthly reason for me to feel anything other than anxiety and despair. It was during those times when that "peace that passes understanding" became real to me.

If we search for an example of such peace in the Old Testament, we need look no further than the situation that the Israelite nation found itself in around the time of Isaiah. Isaiah was a prophet called by God to witness to the nation about its need for repentance. The majority of its people had turned their backs on God, and a time of judgment was coming. Israel had already begun to experience oppression from foreign nations, and the hardships were only going to get worse. Despite the

The Search for Hope

ominous spiritual forecast, Isaiah could speak of God's promise to His hurting people. Isaiah 26:3, 4 states it clearly… "You will keep in perfect peace him whose mind is steadfast, because he trusts in you. Trust in the Lord forever, for the Lord, the Lord, is the Rock eternal."

Just as in Isaiah 26:4, the main requirement of Romans 15:13 is that we trust in God. Admittedly, the requirement of trusting God sometimes feels like climbing Mount Everest with one arm tied behind your back! But if faith as small as a mustard seed can move mountains, then God surely must nod in approval when you make a heartfelt effort to trust Him. The question is…can you take God at His word?

I'm not what you would consider a natural optimist. I try to look at the bright side of things, but it can be exhausting trying to think like that for an entire day. It may be a little easier to do when a day is chugging along perfectly, but a lot harder when that day is full of challenges and frustrations. To imagine that life could *overflow* with good things…well, that really does seem too good to be true. God's directive, so to speak… the clincher…"as you trust in Him", that's the tough part for me. In my years of living, I've learned that there are very few individuals that you can truly trust. You may or may not agree with that statement, but I'm sure you've met untrustworthy people in your life. The lessons learned from those individuals may have been quite painful. The people who hurt you may have been good people who for whatever reason betrayed your trust, or they may have been not so good people who intentionally sought to hurt you. The end result, however, has made you guarded and a bit skeptical about the inherent goodness of your fellow man. God, as all-knowing as He is, took into account the failings of His children when He advised, "It is better to take refuge in the Lord than to trust in man. It is better to take refuge in the Lord than to trust in princes" (Psalm 118: 8-9). There is no one in your life that is more trustworthy and dependable than your loving Father in heaven. While that may seem like a bold assertion, when all else in your life is stripped away, the comfort that comes from accepting that God will never leave you or forsake you is immeasurable.

If you're willing to take that big leap of faith and trust in God's promises, what can you expect? If you follow this verse in Romans further, you'll see that God doesn't wish to supply hope sparingly, but He wants to provide it in quantities that overflow in your life. The word overflow suggests abundance, a plate full with extra servings to spare. You see, God doesn't want to short change what He so lovingly wants to give you! Can you for a moment imagine your life, regardless of current circumstances, filled with the goodness of God's love and mercy…so much so that you welcome each new day as one of endless possibilities in God's wonderful plan for you? Does that have to be too good to be true in your life, or can you accept it as a special, personal gift from the God who wants you to know how precious and loved you are by Him?

The Search for Hope

The hope that God promises…where does it come from more specifically? It's provided to us by the power of the Holy Spirit. While it's invisible to the human eye, it's nevertheless felt in a trusting heart. As Christ's disciples were gifted with the power of the Holy Spirit at Pentecost, so too does the Holy Spirit enter into the hearts of those who are open to God's calling. It may defy human reason, and skeptics may question and even mock the idea, but those who walk in God's will are girded with the undeniable presence of the Holy Spirit. This gift, one so freely given through the sacrificial offering of God's son, Jesus Christ, is the foundation upon which we all can rest for the hope of a truly better tomorrow! My question to you is this, "Can you accept that the God of hope wants to know you personally… that you matter to Him, that He sent His one and only Son to die for you (yes, you!), and that His greatest pleasure comes from having a relationship with you as your loving heavenly Father? If your answer is yes, then you're on your way to finding that true hope which only God can give. If you're still not sure, then please keep reading, because hope for your life doesn't have to be an impossibility!

This book seeks to offer a decidedly different approach to finding hope than what is offered by the world. The search for lasting hope is often a lifelong journey. While we spend energy running after our vision of hope, we need to learn the lesson of letting God's hope find us. Too often we suffer the anguish and doubts that result from the inevitable struggles of human existence. When human strength is gone, and the ability to see anything good in the future has been completely exhausted, it's then that we need to find a new direction. We need to look beyond the questionable wisdom of this world and find the deeper truths for our existence here on earth. The Bible serves as the compass by which we are guided. In it we are privileged to witness the lives of those faithful pilgrims who came before us, those who have persevered by relying on God for all things. By studying how God provided a measure of hope to these individuals, we can gain a measure of comfort and strength as God provides for us in our own lives. What do you hope for in your life? What are those things that you wish you could confidently expect from the Lord? When I think about what I hope for in my life, I guess it comes down to a few basics. I pray that God would keep my loved ones and me safe from harm. That He would provide for my daily needs. That He would safeguard health and well being, and that He would afford me a measure of grace and mercy that would free me from the weight of a very imperfect life. That He would help me walk in His ways. Can God be relied upon for all your needs?

Life represents a challenging and oftentimes painful journey of learning to accept God at His word. Right now you may feel as though there is a vast ocean in front of you, and an approaching storm behind you. You have no boat, no paddle, and treading water has left you exhausted. Your available options are limited. Do you decide to hold on to the hope that God wants to give you, or do you battle the dark churning waters on your own and leave yourself to fate? I pray that despite the burdens you may be carrying right now, you can still believe that hope does exist. Deep down you know there is more to life than just the pain, and that joy and peace can be found if you look for them in the right place.

We need to embrace the truth that God, and God alone, is the source of the only hope that matters in this crazy world of ours. Reaching for a hope apart from Him is wasted effort. Like many things in life, the harder we try to achieve something through our own efforts, the more it escapes our grasp. We were never meant to go it alone. God is there for us. His very intention from the beginning was to "fill us with hope" by the power of the Holy Spirit. Unfortunately, His original plan for us was derailed in the Garden of Eden. But with His help and the help of the Holy Spirit, using the Bible as our guidebook, we can get back on track. When we learn to completely rely on our heavenly Father for all things in our life, especially hope, we'll discover that He can provide for infinitely more than we could ever imagine. My question to you is, "Are you going to focus on the pain of today or the hope of God's tomorrow?"

Chapter 2

HOPE FOR PROTECTION

You are my refuge and my shield; I have put my hope in Your Word.
Psalm 119: 114

As for God, His way is perfect.
All the Lord's promises prove true.
He is a shield for all who look to Him for protection.
2 Samuel 22: 31, NLT

The world can be a scary place. Would you agree with that statement? When we're infants, we rely on our parents to keep us safe. There really is no understanding of protection at that tender age - it's just a given. The physical presence of our parents is a comfort to us in a way that nothing else can be. Our concept of a heavenly father, however, is not very well developed at that age. It's certainly a lot harder to grasp such a concept because God cannot be seen or readily heard. When we're young, the scope of our world is relatively small. Security comes from the conscious and unconscious realization that parents are our guardians. For the most part, children are shielded or largely unaware of the dangers in the world. There's an innocence and naivety that leaves them particularly vulnerable to such dangers, and it is mother, father, sibling or other guardian who makes sure that there is a wall of protection around them.

As we grow older and are exposed to the realities of a fallen world, it becomes increasingly clear that our ability to protect ourselves comes with limitations. When you were younger, did you ever feel that you were indestructible, maybe even invincible? You may have thought to yourself, "Someone my age doesn't get cancer, I won't ever be in an accident, no one will ever rob me or that can't happen to me." The young mind functions differently from that of an adult's, and it seems inconceivable that any of those dangers could actually become reality in that person's life. Talk to a young military recruit who has never tasted battle, and you will appreciate the attitude of invincibility. Compare that to the experiences of a seasoned war veteran and you will quickly appreciate how age and experience can change that confidence in self. As an adolescent, I lost several friends who were close in age to me. While I certainly grieved for them, I could not effectively grasp that they were gone, or that I was not somehow immune to the same fate that they had suffered. One friend had died in a house fire, another in a skiing accident, and another in a car accident. Despite these tragedies, my mind didn't want to accept the losses. Incredibly naïve, but a young brain seems to work that way.

Hope for Protection

As we age, however, each negative event that we or someone else experiences seems to have a greater impact on our lives. When you hear that a friend has been diagnosed with cancer, you no longer think "that can't happen to me". Instead, you wonder what your life would be like if you were the one diagnosed with cancer or another disease. When an acquaintance is out of work because he was injured in a car accident, you start to realize that it could just have easily have happened to you.

As we lose the attitude of invincibility over time, it becomes clearer that our human strength isn't as reliable as we once thought. Our physical frailties make us vulnerable to most of the danger that exists around us. As much as I would still like to believe that I'm in charge of my own destiny, I'm increasingly aware of just how little in control of my life and circumstances that I truly am. Although it's hard to admit, the reality is that without God's protection, life can be an unbearably frightening existence. The real truth is that although unseen, the protection that God affords us throughout each and every day is what keeps us safe when the devil would seek to harm us at every turn.

Since we can't count the number of times that God shields us from danger in any given day, it's easy to buy into the world's argument that God doesn't exist and that we're pretty much on our own. The world wants us to believe that we're rulers of our domain and that it's ridiculous to believe that Satan even exists or is trying to harm us. That's a trap that none of us should fall into. The best way to avoid that trap is to look to

The God of Hope

God's Word and the examples contained within. The Bible has so many instances where God kept His children safe. If God was so good at protecting His loved ones back then, why should we doubt that He would do any less for us today?

One of the early Biblical examples of God's protection is His rescue of the Israelites from the Egyptian army during the exodus. After suffering for many years, the Israelites have finally broken free of their captors. After God sends plague after plague to afflict the Egyptian nation, Pharoah has had enough and finally lets the Israelites leave. Once they're gone, he rethinks the situation and wonders whether he has made a mistake in letting them go. Truth is, the Israelites were the majority of his work force! He decides to go after them. He chases them down and pretty soon the Israelites find themselves trapped between the Egyptian army and the Red Sea. Pharaoh must have been confident that he had his former subjects right where he wanted them. For the Israelites, there was absolutely no route of escape. Human reason would say all hope is lost at this point. After all, there is no armada of ships waiting to ferry the entire Israelite nation to safety. There is also little hope that the nation of Israel, consisting of men, women, children, and livestock, would be able to outrun or outfight what was arguably the most elite fighting force of the time. Yet at the greatest moment of hopelessness for the Israelites, God reassures them by telling Moses, "The Lord will fight for you. You need only to be still." (Exodus 14: 14). Aren't those amazing words? How simple those two sentences are, but just think about what they mean. No one today knows for sure where the Israelites crossed the Red Sea, but out of curiosity, I looked into some theories on the possible location. One research group has speculated that the site of the crossing was the Gulf of Aqaba. The length of the crossing there was estimated by this group to be about 9 miles long. By their calculation, the greatest depth of the sea at one point would have been about 5000 feet. Consider that 5,280 feet equals one mile, and we're talking about slightly less than a mile in depth. Other individuals, however, suggest that a land bridge was formed where the Israelites crossed, and that the depth of the crossing was only about 1000 feet. When you compare that to the height of the Empire State building at 1,250 feet high (not including its antenna!), that wall of water would still have been a terrifying sight for those Israelites. Of course, the exact location or depth of the crossing site shouldn't distract from the real miracle that took place. The real miracle here is that God commanded the waters to part and He made a way for the Israelites to cross. It didn't matter that the mighty Egyptian army was right on their heels. God made sure that the Israelites reached the other side and then He closed the divide. The Egyptian army was caught squarely in the middle of the returning waters and was drowned. The Israelites went from absolutely no hope of escape to complete and utter destruction of their enemy. No wonder that for generations after the exodus, all the nations around Israel referred to their God as the one who brought them out of Egypt.

The God of Hope

No nearby nation would soon forget how the Lord had protected His covenant nation from an army infinitely stronger than it. That by itself should give us great comfort when we are faced with the dangers of this world. When you are overwhelmed by fears that are seen or unseen, please remember those words of Exodus, "The Lord will fight for you. You need only to be still." They are words that the Israelites could rely upon all those thousands of years ago, and they are certainly words that you and I can rely upon in the midst of any and all danger we may face!

Reading through the Old Testament, there is no shortage of examples where God protected his people from dangerous situations. During one period of time, the nation of Israel was at war with the Arameans. Every time the king of Aram made plans to attack Israel, the Israelite prophet Elisha would warn his nation's king, and the attacks would be successfully countered. This enraged the king of Aram, and when he found out that it was Elisha who was responsible for foiling his attack plans, he had his army surround the city where Elisha and his servant were staying. The next morning Elisha's servant looked outside and saw a sea of Aramean horses and chariots. The sight must have terrified him. How could the Israelites stand up against this vast army? Elisha, however, reassured his servant with these words, "Don't be afraid. Those who are with us are more than those who are with them." (2 Kings 6:16) What a statement of confidence in God's ability to protect them! The faith that Elisha demonstrates here is amazing. He knows that the unseen army of

Hope for Protection

God's angels stands ready to act on their behalf. Then Elisha goes one step further. Elisha prays, "O Lord, open his eyes so he may see. Then the Lord opened the servant's eyes, and he looked and saw the hills full of horses and chariots of fire all around Elisha." (2 Kings 6:17). How would you react if you looked out your window one morning and saw that same army of fiery horses and chariots, waiting for the Lord's command to protect you? Would it reassure you, if not leave you completely speechless? Rest assured that as one of God's beloved children, you are no less valuable in His sight than any one person from the nation of Israel! A lot of the time we are just blind to God's protecting forces around us.

In the Old Testament, Hezekiah was king of Judah during some pretty frightening times. Over the years, the nation had been severely weakened because it had turned away from God in order to worship false idols. Their northern neighbor Israel had already been conquered by the newest world power, Assyria. Assyria's king, Sennacherib, was looking to conquer Judah next. In terms of military power, there was no comparison between Assyria and Judah. King Sennacherib's army was the military powerhouse. But King Hezekiah was a godly man. The Bible says of him, "Hezekiah trusted in the Lord, the God of Israel. There was no one like him among the kings of Judah, either before or after him. He held fast to the Lord and did not cease to follow Him; he kept the commands the Lord had given Moses." (2 Kings 18:5-6) Hezekiah relied on the Lord, while

The God of Hope

Sennacherib relied on the strength of his army. After conquering Israel, Sennacherib then went on to overthrow the fortified cities of Judah, leaving the nation even more vulnerable to attack. Following his latest victory, Sennacherib sent his highest ranking officers and army to overthrow the city of Jerusalem. The military commanders taunted the people of Judah with these words, "Hear the word of the great king, the king of Assyria! This is what the king says: Do not let Hezekiah deceive you. He cannot deliver you from my hand. Do not let Hezekiah persuade you to trust in the Lord when he says, 'The Lord will surely deliver us; this city will not be given into the hand of the king of Assyria.'(2 Kings 18: 28-30) Now interrupting the telling of this piece of Biblical history, doesn't this sound familiar to the way of the present day world? When confronted by any number of dangerous situations, can't you hear the world telling you, "You're on your own. There is no God to protect you or bail you out. Don't believe that God loves you…He can't be relied on." I suppose things haven't really changed all that much after so many years. Yet look at Hezekiah's response. What was the first thing he did when he was informed of the threats? He tore his clothes and put on sackcloth as a way of grieving and humbling himself before the Lord. He went to the temple of the Lord and prayed. His officials then went to the prophet Isaiah for guidance, and Isaiah responded, "Tell your master, this is what the Lord says. 'Do not be afraid of what you have heard - those words with which the underlings of the king of Assyria have

Hope for Protection

blasphemed me. Listen! I am going to put such a spirit in him that when he hears a certain report, he will return to his own country, and there I will have him cut down with the sword.'" (2 Kings 19:6-7) Eventually, that's exactly what happened.

Unfortunately, Sennacherib was not ready to give up on his grab for power, so he continued with his threats. And Hezekiah continued with his prayers..."O Lord, God of Israel, enthroned between the cherubim, you alone are God over all the kingdoms of the earth. You have made heaven and earth. Give ear O Lord and hear, open your eyes O Lord and see; listen to the words Sennacherib has sent to insult the living Lord. It is true, O Lord, that the Assyrian kings have laid waste these nations and their lands. They have thrown their gods in to the fire and destroyed them, for they were not gods, but only wood and stone, fashioned by men's hands. Now O Lord our God, deliver us from his hand, so that all kingdoms on earth may know that you alone O Lord are God."(2 Kings 19: 15-19)

Do you see the difference between these two earthly rulers? While Sennacherib elevated himself to a level above all others, and boasted in his own power and might, Hezekiah did just the opposite. He freely acknowledged that God was sovereign and that it was not by earthly power that Judah would be saved. He humbled himself before the Lord and prayed for protection that he knew was directly from God. This is a valuable lesson for us, especially when we try to assume responsibility for the protection of ourselves and our loved ones.

The God of Hope

We don't have the strength necessary to keep us safe from all the threats that arise in any given day. Trying to rely on ourselves can leave us drained of energy and deep in despair. The world and its' daily attacks are simply too much for us to handle on our own.

What happened after Hezekiah prayed? The prophet Isaiah sent this message to the king, "This is what the Lord, the God of Israel, says: I have heard your prayer concerning Sennacherib king of Assyria, he (Sennacherib) will not enter this city or shoot an arrow here. He will not come before it with shield or build a siege ramp against it. By the way he came he will return, he will not enter this city declares the Lord. I will defend this city and save it, for my sake and for the sake of David my servant." (2 Kings 19: 20, 32-34). That very night the Lord sent His angel, who put to death one hundred and eighty five thousand men in the Assyrian camp. When the people of Judah woke the next morning, all they could see were dead bodies. As for Sennacherib, he returned from where he had come, and was later assassinated by his own sons. Not a very pleasant ending for someone who had boasted how powerful he was before God. His behavior lies in stark contrast to Hezekiah, who placed his efforts in praying to the One who was waiting to answer the cries of a humbled and dependent people.

An important point to be made is that God's protection does not depend upon whether or not we deserve it. It isn't affected by how good we are or what we have done to earn it. If

Hope for Protection

you look at Judah's history, the people certainly had not gotten to this point in their national history by following the laws and decrees that God had given them. In fact just the opposite was true. They had repeatedly turned away from God and rightly deserved His hand of judgment. But God was willing to overlook all that because their leader had submitted himself to God and acknowledged the nation's dependence on the only true source of protection...God Himself. And God responded favorably.

Another example of God's protection that I'm particularly fond of is the story of Gideon. I suppose I sympathize with Gideon because he certainly wasn't the bold leader known for his unwavering faith. Gideon was a man who suffered from some serious doubts that kept him from fully believing the Lord's promises. Plus, Gideon's story may just demonstrate how God likes to have a little fun with those who doubt his power and protection. Gideon is what you might call a reluctant warrior, drafted into the defense of his nation when he would have rather run in the opposite direction. I think it's fair to say that he didn't have the boldness of a King David or a Samson.

In what had become a fairly recurrent pattern, the Israelites were being oppressed by their enemy the Midianites, because they had strayed so far from God. They had taken to hiding in caves, and whatever crops they tried to plant were taken or destroyed by the Midianites and other foreign invaders. After seven years of this abuse, the Israelites finally decided to

The God of Hope

ask the Lord for help. God's answer to them was found in Gideon, a man who hid and threshed his wheat in a winepress to keep it hidden from the Midianites. One day God sent his angel to Gideon with the following greeting, "The Lord is with you, mighty warrior." (Judges 6: 12) Gideon might well have looked around for someone else, because it was clear that he didn't consider himself a mighty warrior. After the Lord had told him that he would save Israel from Midian, Gideon's response was this: "But Lord…how can I save Israel? My clan is the weakest in Manasseh, and I am the least in my family." The Lord answered, "I will be with you, and you will strike down all the Midianites, leaving none alive." (Judges 6: 15-16) Gideon was still fairly doubtful, and he wanted more proof than just the Lord's Word. He asked God to use a wool fleece as a sign. First he asked God to prove all this to him by having a wool fleece wet with dew when the rest of the ground was dry. God granted his request. Unfortunately, Gideon still was not convinced, so he asked for the opposite sign. This time he asked God to make the fleece dry and the rest of the ground wet. God patiently complied.

Gideon finally accepted his fate and with his men, a total of 32,000 soldiers, advanced to the Midianite camp. This is where I think the story really gets good. To make sure Israel didn't consider itself solely responsible for any victory against the Midianites, God told Gideon, "You have too many men for Me to deliver Midian into their hands. In order that Israel may not boast against Me that her own strength has saved her, announce to the people, 'Anyone who trembles with fear may turn back and leave Mount Gilead.' (Judges 7: 2-3) Twenty-two thousand men left right then and there. That's a lot of trembling knees! The odds are now stacked against the Israelites, but God isn't finished yet. He tells Gideon that there are still too many men, and orders Gideon to take the men down to the water and to separate them into two groups…those who lapped the water with their tongues like a dog, and those who knelt down to drink. The former group numbered only three hundred men, and this was the group that God chose to fight. He sent the rest of the men home. If your fighting force had gone from thirty-two thousand strong to a mere three hundred men, how confident would you be feeling about your chances for victory? I probably would have been getting my affairs in order, especially since the Midianites were described as being as thick as locusts, and their camels could no more be counted than the sand on the seashore. Gideon must have been showing his fear, for the Lord reassured him by allowing him to overhear the interpretation of a Midianite dream, which described God giving the enemy into Gideon's hands.

    Here was Gideon, along with a few hundred soldiers, and what were they fighting with? In one hand each soldier carried a trumpet, and in the other hand, a torch covered with an empty jar. No bows and arrows, swords, or spears. They were equipped with God's assurance that He would protect and deliver them. Protect them He did. Gideon and his men surrounded the camp, blew their trumpets and broke the jars covering the torches. The Lord then caused the Midianites to turn on each other with their swords, and the Israelites routed their panicked and confused enemy. All of this was accomplished by three hundred men without weapons…because they relied on the Lord to protect them.

Can I ask you, "How protected do you feel right now? Do you feel safe in your current circumstances, or are you feeling particularly vulnerable and exposed?" Often it may feel as if we're being attacked from all sides, with no place to hide. It would be bad enough if you were facing one problem in your life. Perhaps you're struggling with the same financial worries as your friends or neighbors. Maybe you've recently lost your job. That would be challenging enough. But what if there were other challenges in your life that were as bad, if not worse? Maybe you've just been diagnosed with a serious illness. Or maybe you and your spouse are going through a particularly rough patch in your marriage. Whatever it might be, your circumstances have you feeling like you have no safe harbor in the storm. You contemplate available options and realize there's no means of escape. Unlike those classic western movies, there's no cavalry rushing over the hill to save the day." We often live under the mistaken belief that life's problems should be limited in scope and severity. After all, a loving God wouldn't subject us to multiple trials all at once, would He? Isn't a reprieve expected or deserved after surviving one hardship? What happens when that

Hope for Protection

isn't the case? When the hardships never seem to end? It's at that point of submitting to what God allows in our lives that we can understand that our hope in Him endures despite the pain.

King Abijah, one of the kings of Judah, must have known how this felt. Abijah was the grandson of King Solomon, of the royal line of David. He was now ruler over part of a divided kingdom. His father, Rehoboam, was instrumental in creating the division of the Israelite people into northern and southern kingdoms. Jeroboam was the ruler of the northern kingdom Israel, while Abijah ruled over the southern kingdom, Judah. At this point, Judah was still worshiping the Lord, while Israel had taken to worshipping false idols. Ultimately the two kingdoms ended up going to war with one another. Not only was a war bad enough, but what was even worse was that the two sides were fighting against former countrymen. In one particular battle, Jeroboam had sent additional troops to the rear of Judah's army. That way he could ambush Abijah and his men from behind while also attacking from the front. Abijah was definitely getting it from all sides. Second Chronicles describes what happened next: "Judah turned and saw that they were being attacked at both front and rear. Then they cried to the Lord. The priests blew their trumpets and the men of Judah raised the battle cry. At the sound of their battle cry, God routed Jeroboam and all Israel before Abijah and Judah. The Israelites fled before Judah, and God delivered them into their hands. Abijah and his men inflicted heavy losses on them, so that there were five hundred thousand casualties among Israel's able men. The men of Israel were subdued on that occasion, and the men of Judah were victorious because they relied on the Lord, the God of their fathers." (2 Chronicles 13: 14-18) Like the Israelites facing Pharaoh's army at the Red Sea, king Abijah faced overwhelming odds. Yet as we read in both accounts, amazing things happen when we place our trust in the Lord to protect us!

All these examples are from Biblical times, and you might be justified in asking how these instances relate to our present day lives. Some might make the argument that the world is a much different place than it was back then. That may be true, but if you really look, you'll find that the Lord's hand is still as capable of protection, if perhaps a little more subtly than in Old Testament times.

Several years ago there was a story in the news that spoke to God's use of the uncommon to protect one of His children. I'm an animal lover, so any time I hear a story that involves animals and has a spiritual nature to boot, my interest is peaked. This story involved a twelve year old girl in Ethiopia. It seems that she was abducted and beaten by a group of tribesmen who intended great physical and emotional harm to her. As expected, this girl was seriously outnumbered by these men and had no hope of escape or rescue, as she was in an isolated area of the country. Suddenly out of the bush a number of lions appeared, seemingly from nowhere, and chased off the men. These lions physically surrounded and protected this girl for

Hope for Protection

about half a day, making sure that no one came near her until she was rescued by the local authorities. When the police showed up, the lions disappeared back into the bush. "They stood guard until we found her, and then they just left her like a gift and went back into the forest", one of the rescuing policemen reported. This story was reported by a secular news agency, and one of their explanations for this amazing incident was that the lions didn't harm the girl because her cries were mistaken for a distressed lion cub. For any person of faith, though, the explanation is all too clear. God opened His hand, and in a way that only He could do, protected this young girl when there was no ordinary means of protection to be found.

Does this modern day story of protection remind you of another one from the Bible? One has only to think back to the story of Daniel and the lion's den in the Old Testament. Daniel had been set up by some devious officials in the court of King Darius. What was his crime? He was unwilling to bow down and worship the false gods of the Babylonian nation. As punishment, he was ordered to be thrown into a den of hungry lions. Daniel's death seemed imminent, but God closed the mouths of the lions and Daniel was kept safe until he was brought out of the pit.

How often do we read the Biblical accounts of miracles and yet are still skeptical about God being able to act in similar ways today? God closed the mouths of the lions to protect Daniel those thousands of years ago. Here in this modern day account, God not only closed the mouths of the lions but used those same lions to protect a vulnerable child from harm. God is still working His miracles today. We just need to be willing to see them.

Have you ever been in a situation where your life was at risk, and you knew you were in real trouble? It may have been a scary encounter in a car or on a deserted city street, but you knew that danger was all around. Yet somehow you escaped the situation unhurt and it left you realizing that a greater force was working on your behalf. Could you imagine what it would be like to jump from a plane and then discover that your parachute wasn't working? That's exactly what happened to one young woman. On October 9, 2005, Shayna Richardson was a twenty-one year old skydiver making her first solo jump from a plane in Arkansas. That day is one she would never forget. As she jumped from the plane and tried to open her main parachute, she soon realized that it was malfunctioning. As she was falling, she was able to cut that chute away so that the reserve chute could open. The only problem was that the reserve chute failed as well. There she was, plummeting out of the sky and accelerating toward the ground below. She ended up hitting the asphalt of a parking lot face first at fifty miles per hour. And she survived! There were broken bones and multiple surgeries, but she recovered enough to even be able to skydive again! To make this miracle even more amazing, Shayna learned in the hospital right after the fall that she was pregnant… and her baby survived as well! Months later, she gave birth to a healthy baby boy, with no

Hope for Protection

ill effects from the accident. As Shayna described it, "So not only did God save me but He spared this baby." It would be pretty hard to doubt God's hand in this rescue, wouldn't it?

Intellectually we know that God is there to protect us, but sometimes in the depths of despair, we can have a hard time acknowledging that fact. If you fall into this category at times, the one thing I can say is take heart, because you and I are in good company. Often we doubt because we can't physically see God. But when you feel like beating yourself up over this seeming lack of faith, take comfort in knowing that those before you suffered from the same doubts.

Imagine what it must have been like to be one of Jesus' disciples. Think for a moment how it would feel to stand witness to all of the miracles that Jesus performed…healing the blind and lame, changing water into wine, feeding the hungry to name just a few. You could see with your own eyes that Jesus was who He said He was. There should have been no doubt as to what Jesus was capable of. But there was. In the book of Mark, Jesus and the disciples were in a boat, crossing over to the other side of the lake after a full day spent with a local crowd of people. While they were crossing, a storm came up and the waves were so rough they almost swamped the boat. The disciples were terrified, afraid that they were soon to meet their end. Where was Jesus? He was in the stern of the boat, asleep! The disciples woke Him in their terror, and had this to say to Him…"Teacher, don't you care if we drown?" (Mark 4: 38) To the disciples, even the physical presence of Jesus did little to reassure them that they would be protected. Jesus obviously wasn't concerned, because He was fast asleep. To these doubting disciples, that must have made the situation seem all the more dire. Didn't Jesus care enough about them to save them from the storm? Of course we know He did, but the disciples' perspective was skewed by the danger around them. When Jesus got up, "He rebuked the wind and said to the waves, 'Quiet, be still!' Then the wind died down and it was completely calm" (Mark 4: 39). Just like that, with one command from the Son of God, the storm was over. Jesus had some choice words for His disciples afterward. "Why are you so afraid? Do you still have no faith?" How about you and me? Can we say we will trust that God will protect us from every danger, even when we can't see Him?

You may not be the seafaring type, so perhaps you have never been in the middle of a body of water when a storm has come up. But have you ever suddenly found yourself in the midst of a fast moving summer thunderstorm? Where it seems that one moment there is just the diffuse gray of an overcast sky, and the next moment the wind has kicked up with a monsoon like downpour, and the thunder and lightning alternate in relentless fury? I have been through more than my fair share of these types of storms, and each one leaves me feeling exposed and extremely vulnerable. It's a very unsettling feeling, and one that reminds me just how small I am and how big God's universe is. However frightening the storm, be it an actual one with wind and water or a figurative one that leaves us feeling battered and defenseless, never forget that God has the final say in His universe. As Jesus commanded the wind to be still, so our heavenly Father provides the safe refuge for us through any storm that we may be facing.

You see, every one of us has been given a life that is part of God's plan for the world. We may think that we matter very little in the grand scheme of things, but God has made a place for each and every one of His children in the history of this world. We are all alive for a reason, and you can be sure that God's hand of protection will cover you while you are living out your life for Him. When God has a job for you to do, no one will be able to break through the barrier of his protection to prevent you from accomplishing your purpose. Consider King David and all that he went through on his way to becoming king of the Israelite nation. David's predecessor, King Saul, had failed in his responsibilities to God and the Israelites. God had made it clear that the throne would be taken away from Saul and given to David. God's decision, however, did not sit well with Saul. He wasn't ready to give up the throne. As devoted as David had been to the king, Saul tried multiple times to have David killed. Yet whenever the opportunity arose for David to take the life of Saul, he declined to do it. Although Saul had the greater resources, David was part of God's plan for leadership of His people. In the end, it was David's life that was spared and Saul's life that was taken. God wanted David as king, and king he became. Or consider the life of Saint Paul. In the book of Acts, Paul is a Roman prisoner on board a ship bound for Italy. An angel of the Lord had appeared to Paul on the journey and told him that he must stand trial before Caesar. The only problem was that the rest of the journey had to take place during the most dangerous time of the year for sea voyages. For fourteen days Paul and the other passengers aboard the ship battled the rough seas. Then, the ship struck a sandbar and was destroyed. All two hundred seventy-six passengers survived. The soldiers aboard the ship were worried that the prisoners would escape in the confusion, so they were thinking about killing Paul and the other prisoners. Their centurion intervened, however, and again Paul's life was spared. Now safely on the shores of Malta, the local islanders built a fire for the survivors. As Paul was gathering firewood, he was bitten by a deadly snake. Instead of becoming sick and dying, Paul suffered no ill effects from the snakebite, much to the amazement of those around him. Most of us know the contributions that Paul made in advancing the Gospel message through his many travels. But he could not have had such an impact without God's protection. Shipwreck, attempted murder, and venomous snake could not stop the plan that God had put into place for Paul's life.

    If you're still questioning God's willingness to protect you, take a look at one of the most profound and comforting psalms in the Old Testament…Psalm 91. Everything about this psalm points to a loving God who wants us to turn to Him in

Hope for Protection

every dangerous and frightening circumstance. Each verse speaks directly to the heart. "If you make the Most High your dwelling- even the Lord, who is my refuge- then no harm will befall you, no disaster will come near your tent." (Psalm 91: 9-10) Using the analogy of a protective mother hen, verse four is perhaps the most reassuring of all. "He will cover you with His feathers, and under His wings you will find refuge; His faithfulness will be your shield and rampart." Anyone who has worked with animals or even poultry knows that the protective instinct of a mother is one of the strongest forces in nature. A mother's devotion to her young knows no limits and she will risk her own life for the safety of her offspring. I can remember reading about someone who was surveying the damage done to the landscape after a particularly destructive forest fire. This person had come across the charred body of a bird at the base of a tree. Upon closer inspection, he noticed that under her wings, there were chicks that had survived the fire. That mother had given her life to protect the lives of her chicks. As amazing as that is, just consider for a moment who we are in the eyes of God. Flawed as we might be, the love that God has for us is limitless. The God of hope, the One who created the heavens and the earth, loves us so much that He was willing to sacrifice His one and only Son in order to save us! It's not anything we needed to earn: His love is given as a free gift to each and every one of us. No strings attached! Every single day of our lives, God wants to be the One we run to, so that we can find shelter

The God of Hope

and protection in His everlasting arms, much like those chicks found safety under their mother's wings. What a comforting thought!

Chapter 3

HOPE FOR PROVISION

*The eyes of all look to You, and You give them
their food at the proper time.*
Psalm 145: 15

*And my God will meet all your needs according to His glorious
riches in Christ Jesus.*
Philippians 4: 19

When you're a child, pretty much all of your physical needs are provided for by your parents. During those early years, you don't tend to focus on what your needs are or who will meet them. You just instinctively understand that your parents will provide what you need when you need it. As you mature into an adult, however, more and more of what was your parents' responsibility now gets shifted onto your shoulders. That can be stressful enough. Then add the responsibility of caring and providing for a family, and those shoulders really begin to get weighed down. You work longer hours and think about getting a second job, but nothing seems to get any easier. Suddenly the economy takes a nosedive, the office starts laying off workers, and you begin to worry a little more than usual. Media outlets report that the unemployment rate is creeping up again, more jobs are being shipped overseas, health care costs are rising, and every government entity is raising taxes to make up for the perpetual budgetary shortfall. Somehow, your hopes for an easier tomorrow just flew out the window.

When the economic forecast looks bleak, where do you turn for help? It's only natural, I suppose, to try to brainstorm a way out of any financial hole by yourself. You can rely on your own resources, as meager as they may be, and hope that they're enough to cover the bills at the end of the month. You can turn to family or friends for help. Maybe you're hoping a rich long-lost uncle pops up who is willing to write out a big check that will solve all your financial problems. Then there's always the lottery, because it seems a lot of hopes and dreams are placed on hitting those lucky numbers. But what if those options aren't enough or aren't available? Would you consider turning to God for help? He has, after all, promised to provide for us. In Philippians 4:19, St. Paul writes, "And my God will meet all your needs according to His glorious riches in Christ Jesus". That's a pretty confident statement in God's abilities, isn't it? Could God actually mean <u>everything</u> we need? Could you imagine what peace this one verse would bring if only we could believe it? There's a saying that I've embraced during some fairly lean years in my life. It says "If you have been reduced to God being your only hope, you are in a good place". How good is the place that you're in right now? Would you be willing to

Hope for Provision

accept that God wants to be the first one you turn to for every possible need?

Can we *really* rely on God to provide all that we need for our daily lives? Are the words in the Lord's Prayer something we can truly take to heart…"Give us this day our daily bread"? And what exactly is that daily bread we're hoping God will provide? I particularly like the explanation that Martin Luther offers in his "Small Catechism". Our daily bread includes "everything that has to do with the support and needs of the body, such as food, drink, clothing, shoes, house, home, land, animals, money, goods, a devout husband or wife, devout children, devout workers, devout and faithful rulers, good government, good weather, peace, health, self-control, good reputation, good friends, faithful neighbors and the like". That's quite a list, isn't it?

Our daily bread includes all things that the Lord knows we need to live the life that He has intended for us. Even before we cry out to Him with our need, God knows our situation and what is necessary to keep us well supplied. As Luther so beautifully explains, "God tenderly invites us to believe that He is our true Father and that we are His true children, so that with all boldness and confidence we may ask Him as dear children ask their dear father".

Our parents' responsibility to provide for us may have been met as we reached adulthood, but rest assured that our heavenly Father's responsibility to provide for us knows no age limits. From the day of our birth to the day of our death, He is the ultimate provider of our every need. If you're still not quite convinced of that, then maybe a good place to start would be to look to the Bible for some reassuring examples of how God provided for His children.

God's very first act of provision for mankind began with Adam and Eve. There in the Garden of Eden, Adam and Eve had everything they could possibly need or want. It was all generously given to them, that is, until their eyes got a little bigger than they should have, and the smooth talking serpent convinced them that what God had given them was not enough. In spite of their sin and despite their eviction from this earthly version of paradise, God didn't stop providing for them.

A little farther along in the book of Genesis, we're introduced to Abraham, whose name means the father of many nations. The only problem with having a name like that was that Abraham had no heir who was going to be the beginning of any nation. Abraham was a righteous man, however, and he believed God when he was told in a vision that his offspring would be as numerous as the stars in the heavens. Despite the fact that Abraham and his wife were beyond the typical childbearing years, God provided them with their first born son, Isaac. Imagine how Abraham must have felt, all but having given up on fatherhood, and then being blessed with an heir! How he must have loved that child. Yet as often happens, circumstances in life can cause us to doubt God's presence and willingness to provide.

Hope for Provision

Some years later, God instructed Abraham to sacrifice his son Isaac. The question Abraham must have asked himself was, "Why?" Why would God finally bless him with a son, only to then ask Abraham to take the life of that child? As painful as this must have been for Abraham, he didn't resist. There on one of the mountains of Moriah, Abraham readied himself for this painful sacrifice. When Isaac, unaware of his fate, asked his father where the lamb for the burnt offering was, Abraham replied that God Himself would provide. What faith this righteous man of God must have had! Most of us know what happened after that. God, in His infinite mercy, didn't allow Abraham to go through with the sacrifice. Instead, God provided a ram, caught by its horns in a nearby thicket, for the burnt offering. What did Abraham call the place where this took place? "The Lord Will Provide". Oh, that you and I might have a fraction of the faith that Abraham had at that moment…to know with unwavering certainty that God will provide for every need, great or small, that we have in this life!

God's promise to Abraham, that he would be the father of many nations, certainly came true. Several hundred years after Abraham's death, however, the people of Israel found themselves in the untenable position of being slaves in Egypt. These descendants of Abraham now knew what it meant to experience want and hardship. Despite their difficulties, God was working behind the scenes to provide an escape for them. God chose Moses to lead his people out of Egypt, and nowhere was

The God of Hope

God's hand of provision more obvious that in this nation's mass exodus.

God's promise to the downtrodden nation was that He would lead them to a land flowing with milk and honey. For these poor helpless souls, that must have sounded too good to be true. I imagine anything would have been better than the situation they were in. So when Moses led that mass of humanity out of Egypt, there was much to look forward to. In fact, God worked it in such a way that the people of Egypt actually handed over their possessions to the Israelites. That fulfilled what God had told Abraham so many years before, "But I will punish the nation they serve as slaves, and afterward they will come out with great possessions." (Genesis 15: 14) Can't you just picture the Egyptians lined up all along the road, as the Israelites marched out of town in one grand procession, carrying their newly acquired "gifts"? Exodus 12:36 sums it up in a nutshell…"The Lord had made the Egyptians favorably disposed toward the people, and they gave them whatever they asked for, so they plundered the Egyptians." I can envision those same generous Egyptians, the day after the exodus, wondering what on earth had just happened when they realized they had given away the "general store"!

Once out in the desert, the situation changed quite a bit for the newly freed Israelites. Because of their rebellious attitude toward God, a trip that was to take but a few years became one that would last forty years. The task of feeding a nation that size,

Hope for Provision

for that long a period of time, became a much greater challenge. Despite the people's grumbling, God responded with a characteristic generosity that is amazing even to this day. He had manna rain down from heaven to feed the people each morning. For the length of this journey, the Israelites could rely on a daily supply of this "bread of heaven". In the evening, God provided them with quail in such numbers they couldn't be counted. Did the people deserve such merciful treatment? Probably not, but you see, God's provision is based on His mercy, not our merit. Can you recall a time or two in your childhood when you didn't particularly care for what was waiting for you at the dinner table? Rather than be grateful that there was food to eat instead of going without, you may have grumbled to your parents about the menu. If your mom and dad were like most parents, you might even have heard the following- "If you don't like what's on your plate, you can head to your room with an empty stomach!" Despite their shortcomings, God demonstrated amazing patience towards His children. He provided for them even when their gratitude was in short supply. Many years later, Nehemiah spoke of God's generosity during those forty years to the Jewish exiles who had returned home from Babylon. "Because of Your (God's) great compassion You did not abandon them in the desert. By day the pillar of cloud did not cease to guide them on their path, nor the pillar of fire by night to shine on the way they were to take. You gave Your good Spirit to instruct them. You did not withhold Your manna from their mouths, and You gave them water for their thirst. For forty years You sustained them in the desert; they lacked nothing, their clothes did not wear out nor did their feet become swollen" (Nehemiah 9: 19-21). Does that give you a little bit of hope, knowing that God is willing to provide for us even when we may not deserve it?

While the examples above clearly demonstrate God's willingness to provide for our needs, there are also times when it seems that God may have forgotten us. In the Old Testament book of second Kings, we read about a widow who was in a desperate situation after the death of her husband. In Old Testament times, the loss of a husband often meant that the means of support for the family was gone. Such must have been the case for this widow with two sons. The widow confronts the prophet Elisha and tells him that her God-fearing husband is dead, and that his creditor is coming to take away her two sons as slaves. Can there be anything more heartbreaking for this woman than losing her boys after already losing her husband?

God, of course, is working through Elisha in all of this. Elisha asks this woman what he can do for her, and specifically wants to know what she has in her house. The widow replies that she has nothing but a little oil. Here is where the story gets interesting. Elisha then tells this woman to go ask her neighbors for some empty jars. He doesn't tell her to ask for just one or two jars, however. He wants her to find as many as she can. Are you starting to get an inkling of where this is leading? Elisha tells her that once she has gotten the jars, she is to go inside and shut the door behind her and her sons. He further instructs her to pour oil into each jar, and when each jar is filled, to set it aside. The widow obediently complies with his order, and that little bit of oil fills each and every jar. When all the jars have been filled, she asks her sons for one more, but they tell her there aren't any more. Only when the last jar had been filled did the oil stop flowing. Elisha instructs her to sell the oil and pay her debts, so that she and her sons can live on the money left over.

I'd say it was a safe bet that when that poor widow woke up that morning, she had no idea what the Lord had in store for her that day. To her, the day would unfold with more hardship and heartbreak. Never in her wildest dreams could she have imagined the miracle that was waiting for her and her sons. But that is at the heart of who God is…He is ever watchful, and His hand of provision can come at a time when the situation you may be facing seems the most hopeless. Had that widow been able to find twice the number of jars to fill with oil, I have no doubt that God would have kept the oil flowing to fill them.

A similar situation involved another prophet of God…Elijah. At first, Elijah is the one who is on the receiving end of God's provision. Then God uses him to provide relief to another suffering widow. Elijah had just finished warning King Ahab that a drought was soon coming to the land occupied by Israel. As you can imagine, King Ahab wouldn't have been too happy to hear this. The Lord tells Elijah to leave where he is and to hide east of the Jordan River, which he does. The Lord tells Elijah, "You will drink from the brook, and I have ordered the ravens to feed you there." (1 Kings 17: 4) Twice a day, the ravens brought Elijah bread and meat to eat. Can you picture yourself being waited on by birds? God, however, is not limited by the laws of nature. He created the laws of nature! He can use man, beast or bird to carry out His will, even if His ways are beyond anything we could possibly imagine or understand.

Once the predicted drought arrived, Elijah was instructed to head to the town of Zarephath, where God tells Elijah that he has commanded a widow there to supply him with food. Elijah is probably thinking that that sounds a bit more reasonable than being fed by ravens. When he arrives in town and finds the widow, he asks her for a drink of water and a piece of bread. Her reply to him, however, was probably not what Elijah had expected to hear. She tells him, "As surely as the Lord your God lives…I don't have any bread – only a handful of flour in a jar and a little oil in a jug. I am gathering a few sticks to take home and make a meal for myself and my son that we may eat it and die." (1 Kings 17: 12) If God could provide Elijah with food from birds, why on earth would He now send the prophet to a widow who has no food to offer? I think the lesson here is that no situation is beyond the power of God. He can turn the most hopeless of situations around. Elijah tells the widow not to be afraid, and to go home and do as she had said. But first he asks her to make a small cake of bread for him from the little flour

Hope for Provision

and oil she has. She was to bring it to Elijah, and then make something for her son and herself. Then she hears the most reassuring words from Elijah's lips, "For this is what the Lord, the God of Israel, says: 'The jar of flour will not be used up and the jug of oil will not run dry until the day the Lord gives rain on the land.'" If you hardly had any food left, wouldn't you be reluctant to give your last portion to a complete stranger? Yet this woman obeyed Elijah's instructions, and the flour and oil didn't run out, just as God had promised through the prophet.

The significance of what happened to these two widows is that they had both exhausted their own resources. Their position was at the bottom rung of society's ladder, and there was no one willing or able to help them or their children. Surely nothing is more hopeless than when you are completely powerless to solve your own problems. These women were at the end of their proverbial rope. They must have prayed for help for days, if not months, only to be met with seeming silence from God. At the very last hour, a miracle occurred that changed their immediate situation and provided hope. That miracle must have changed their mindset and engraved on their hearts the mercy and providence of a loving God. What can these widows teach us today, in whatever situation of want we may find ourselves in? That we must never give up hope, because no matter how bleak tomorrow looks, God can always make a way.

During those Old Testament times, God often provided for his people sight unseen, or used his prophets to carry out His will. In the New Testament, it was often Jesus or His disciples who directly intervened on behalf of the people. One of the most memorable examples of Jesus providing for the people was when He fed the five thousand.

At the time, Jesus was grieving the murder of His cousin John the Baptist. He had tried to get away to the remote town of Bethsaida, but the local crowds had followed Him. In spite of His grief, the Bible says He had compassion on the people and healed their sick. By the end of that day, everyone was hungry. The disciples tried to convince Jesus to send the people away to the villages to buy their own food. Jesus had other plans. He told the disciples to feed the crowd. Unfortunately, the disciples had only five loaves of bread and two fish. How many were in the crowd that day? The Bible says that the number of those who ate were about five thousand men, besides women and children. Can you just picture the look on the disciples' faces as they try to figure out how they're going to feed that many people with such a small amount of food? Jesus wasn't the least concerned. He had the disciples bring Him the food, and the first thing He did was give thanks to His Father in heaven. He acknowledged that everything comes from the Father. He then broke the loaves and gave them and the fish to the disciples, who passed them out to the people. All the people ate until they were fully satisfied, and the disciples then collected all the food that was left. From those two fish and five loaves, the disciples collected twelve basketfuls

Hope for Provision

of leftovers (Matthew 14: 13-21). When God supplies, He does so abundantly!

Jesus repeats this miraculous event when He feeds another crowd of four thousand men, not including women and children. This time, He has seven loaves of bread and a few small fish…still not nearly enough to feed a crowd that size. But He knows that the people who have come to Him are hungry. They have spent the last three days with Him as He healed them of their illnesses. He tells His disciples, "I do not want to send them away hungry, or they may collapse on the way." (Matthew 15:32) It would have been easy for Jesus to have turned His back on them, and let them fend for themselves. But He isn't like that. His compassion is evident in the way that He responds to the situation. Just as He was willing to show infinite mercy to all those people back then, He wants to be as generous to us today.

Can you imagine what a miracle like that would look like today? Suppose that you had decided to volunteer at a homeless shelter, say after a recent natural disaster. On a normal day, there are more than enough people in real need. On this particular day, the lines of the hungry are stretched down city blocks for as far as you can see. You're in charge of the kitchen today, so you set about trying to organize the supplies for cooking. You open the door to the shelter kitchen and get a sick feeling in your gut. The pantry shelves are bare, except for a couple of loaves of bread. The inside of the refrigerator doesn't look any more promising…only a few hamburger patties sitting

The God of Hope

lonely on the shelves. Once you get over the initial shock, you try to suppress the sense of panic that's welling up inside you. Being a person of faith, you take a deep breath and pray, "Lord, please provide, and thank you for the blessings You have given us." Admittedly, you know that God can do anything, because the Bible has shown you that, but you can't help but be a little doubtful. After all, just how many people are waiting outside? You come to the conclusion that maybe you can't feed them all, but you can at least feed a few, and that's better than nothing. You fire up the grill and start slicing the bread. Then a curious thing happens. You go to take the slices of bread and put them in a basket, and as you turn back around you notice another loaf of bread sitting right where the last one had been. You think to yourself, "That's odd". At the moment there's no one else in the kitchen, so it couldn't have been someone else putting it there. You shrug it off, thinking you're tired and imagining things. Well, this is definitely the last loaf now. Yet when you place this loaf in the basket and turn back around, there's another loaf staring right back at you! What would you be thinking at this point? That you're hallucinating? Or could this be God actually providing the food for which you had prayed? For as long as you keep slicing bread, more bread appears. Now it's time for the hamburger patties. Each time you take a patty off the grill, another one appears in its place. This goes on for hours. Your fellow shelter volunteers have all come to watch this incredible phenomenon, and no one knows what to say. You can't all be hallucinating, can you? By the end of that day, every single person in that shelter has been fed, with leftover food to spare. Would anyone who wasn't there that day believe you when you tried to tell them what had happened? Those people getting fed only know that there was food for them when they so desperately needed it. To them, God did provide, but not necessarily in the miraculous way that you know He did. To you and your colleagues, that day would be one you're not likely to forget.

    These two acts of Jesus feeding the massive crowds are what I like to think of as "big ticket" items. Feeding thousands of people with a few loaves and fishes is a pretty big deal. Yet, even in the smaller needs of those around Him, He showed that He could be relied upon. In His earliest documented miracle, Jesus and His disciples had been invited to a wedding in Galilee. This was a time of celebration, until a small crisis arose when the host ran out of wine. Jesus' mother, who was also present, informed Him of the shortage. His reply to His mother might seem harsh by today's standards…"Dear woman, why do you involve me?" (John 2: 4). Undeterred by His seeming callousness and disinterest, she tells the servants, "Do whatever He tells you." (John 2: 5). She knows her son well enough to know that He won't let her down. Jesus instructs the servants to take six water jars (each holding from twenty to thirty gallons) and fill them to the brim with plain water, which He proceeds to change into wine! The servants obey, and He then tells them to draw some of this new wine out of the jars and take it to the master of the banquet. The master tastes the sample, not knowing where it has come from. He's so impressed by the quality of this vintage that he pulls the bridegroom aside and says to him, "Everyone brings out the choice wine first and then the cheaper wine after the guests have had too much to drink; but you have saved the best till now. (John 2: 10) Not only had Jesus turned ordinary water into wine, but He made sure that its quality was first rate. When God provides, He doesn't cut corners.

One of the smaller miracles that Jesus performed is also one of my personal favorites…for two reasons. First, to me it shows that Jesus had a slight sense of humor. Second, it's a reminder that although Jesus wants to provide for our needs, there are times when we have to put in a little legwork as well. Jesus and His disciples had just arrived in Capernaum. No sooner had they set foot in town, the local tax collectors confronted Peter (things haven't changed much since then, have they?) and asked him, "Doesn't your teacher pay the temple tax?" (Matthew 17: 24). Peter replied yes, and promptly headed off to update Jesus on what had just taken place. Before Peter could say a word, Jesus was already giving him a lesson in taxes…He's way ahead of His disciple. Not wanting to defy the tax collectors, He informed Peter that they would each pay the two drachma tax. Now they only need to come up with the money. After feeding all those thousands of people, it would have been a simple matter for Jesus to have produced the necessary funds on the spot. What did Jesus do instead? He told

Hope for Provision

Peter, "Go to the lake and throw out your fishing line. Take the first fish you catch; open its mouth and you will find a four drachma coin. Take it and give it to them for my tax and yours." Why does Jesus send Peter on this aquatic scavenger hunt? Perhaps it was to have a little fun with Peter, or perhaps it was to see if Peter really believed that Jesus would provide for what was needed. While Jesus certainly could have handed him a coin right then and there, He creates the most unlikely scenario in which to find God's provision. I suppose that may have been Jesus' way of assuring Peter that it could only have come from the Lord. Either way, the need was a real one, and Jesus met it in unforgettable fashion!

At this point you may be thinking that while it's nice to focus on the miracles of the Old and New Testaments, they are less relevant to your situation today. The way in which God provided for His people all those years ago is probably not going to apply to the needs you may be facing today. At least the last time you checked, your kitchen refrigerator had not mysteriously been stocked with food, and no one had miraculously paid your rent or mortgage for the month. Might it be possible that God is still providing for us in magnificent ways? Could it be that we have just lost our awareness of the ways in which God intervenes on our behalf? It certainly is much easier to question God's provision when we focus on everything the world tells us we need but don't have. It's undeniable that poverty and want exist in every nation of the world. But if you or I were to really get

The God of Hope

serious about what we have been blessed with in our lives, would our vision of God's provision become any clearer?

Each of us is left to answer that last question on our own, as we all have had different life experiences that have formed our opinions. For me, I've realized with each passing year that God is always willing to provide, as long as I look to Him for the answer. Two small incidents in my own life reinforced that truth for me. While trivial in the grand scheme of things, each reassured me of the Lord's hand of provision in even the smallest of needs.

The first incident occurred during my college years and left no doubt in my young mind that God's hand was involved. During my undergraduate days I lived in a residence hall on campus. Each year a lottery was conducted to see if you would keep your room or if you had to give it up to someone else. I was a relatively shy student, and I had grown to love my little dorm room. I had made good friends on the hallway and that dorm room had that little sense of home away from home. At the end of my second year, the lottery was held and to my horror, I lost out. That now meant that I would have to find a new place to live. When I look back on that time and consider some of the real trials I have had to face since then, it doesn't seem like that much of a hardship. But at the time, it seemed catastrophic. I didn't want to move and give up what I had become so accustomed to. I didn't want to have to leave my friends and dorm mates behind. I remember being upset of course, and although there were much

Hope for Provision

more important matters to be approaching God with, I felt in this instance I would really lay my burden down at His feet and engage Him in prayer. I remember reading a phrase that has stuck with me for many years…"If it matters to you, it matters to Him". Boy did this matter! There were any number of ways that God could have handled the situation, but the way He chose to deal with it is something I still remember with unmistakable clarity twenty five years later. It seemed that there was a flaw in the computer program that ran the lottery. As a result, it was determined that the lottery process was not as random an event as it should have been. Since fairness couldn't be verified, the administrators decided that every student would be able to remain in their dorm room for another year if they wanted to. To anyone else, this certainly was not an earthshaking answer to a monumental problem, but to me it made all the difference in the world. It reaffirmed to me, as a still immature Christian, the amazing ways that God works in our lives. What doesn't make a difference to one person can mean the world to another person. It doesn't matter how small the request, or how seemingly hopeless the situation is. God can make a way, and He can most certainly provide. The important thing is that we acknowledge that He alone is the source of everything we need in this life. We're dependent on a loving Father who wishes to supply our needs…physical, emotional, spiritual and everything in between.

The second incident involves another small event, but underscores just how much God wants us to rely on Him for everything. I will start by saying that it does involve a material possession. I'm in no way suggesting or advocating that anyone should approach God with their needs as if He were a "magic genie". God is sovereign, and as such we are to approach Him with the awe and fearful reverence that the Bible instructs us to. My point in relaying this episode is that there is nothing so small in a person's life that it doesn't matter to our heavenly Father.

If anyone were to ask, I would describe myself as a fairly practical person. I live a simple life, and am pretty well satisfied with having the basic necessities of life met. When buying things, I always think of the utility of the object in question. That being said, although I will make purchases based on practicality, I will also let my mind wander when something catches my eye. Case in point…I have only owned two new cars in my life. The first new car that I purchased was a little station wagon that I absolutely adored. One of the newer features of the car's radio was that when you were playing cassettes (I'm aging myself here!), you could press a button and have your favorite song play over and over again. Like I said, little things make me happy! After eleven years and over 220,000 miles, it became clear that it was time to go car shopping again. I did some research and started scanning the roads for any cars that looked to fit my needs and budget. I noticed one particular model on the road that seemed to fit what I was looking for. The next stop was a visit to the local dealership. The car was about as reasonably priced for its class as one might expect. This particular car had

Hope for Provision

both a basic model and a sport model. The sport model had a zippy royal blue stripe down the middle of the console and this nifty sunroof. I had never owned a car with a sunroof before, but sunroofs were one of those non-necessities that caught my eye. I could just imagine myself driving down the road with the sunroof open and the fresh air spilling in! Of course the sport model cost twelve hundred dollars more than the base model and that was a deal breaker as far as I was concerned. So I really didn't even consider that model because it didn't fit into my budget or sense of practicality. There were at least a dozen better uses for that money than a sunroof, provided I even had an extra twelve hundred dollars to spend. I really do believe that God knows the smallest desires of our hearts, though. I would never have even considered approaching God for something like that because it was materialistic and silly at the same time. It definitely wasn't a legitimate need and I knew that. But without me even verbalizing it to God, I believe He knew my heart's desire and acted on it. As it turned out, the base model I was looking at was not in stock, and the dealer offered me the next model up at the same price! You guessed it, the next model up was the sport model with the bright blue stripe on the console and the great sunroof. I'm still driving that car today, and it is a frequent reminder of God's provision in matters so small that I might not even dare to ask Him. It represents the assurance that the Lord knows my innermost desires whether I approach Him with them or not. He loves us so much that He goes out of His way to show us…"Yes, you are my child and I want to provide for you. I want you to depend on Me, and I want you to look to Me for everything. You can rest in the knowledge that I will not abandon you or leave you wanting." God wants to be involved in every aspect of your life. When the bills are due or the other needs of this life seem like they are going to smother you, hold on to your own memories of how God has provided for you in the past. They will help to keep you on the path of faith and help squash those seeds of doubt trying to grow in your heart.

When I look back over the years of my life and try to think of a time when God did not provide for my real needs, I'm hard pressed to come up with one. That certainly is not to say that God has always made things easy for me. That's not the case at all. There have been periods in my life where I have been at the point of despair, wondering whether I would have the money to pay the bills, or whether the right job would come along. But when I'm really honest with myself, the difficulties that I had during those times were more related to my lack of faith in God's ability to provide, rather than in God's actual willingness or power to provide. Then again, there is often a distinction that should be made between what we truly need versus what we would like to have in this life. Has God blessed you and your family with enough food to make it through the week? It may not be steak and caviar…in fact it may be mac and cheese, or seven different versions of spaghetti, but it was enough to ensure that no one in your home went hungry. Do you have a roof over your

Hope for Provision

head? Maybe it leaks a little during a heavy rain, or the living space is a bit cramped for the size of your family, but you still can call it home in spite of it all. The point is that when we can focus on what we have been blessed with, instead of what's missing in our lives, God's hand of provision becomes that much clearer to see.

If you're like the majority of people, the fact that God has provided for your needs in the past doesn't necessarily reassure you that He will continue to do so in the future. I can sheepishly admit that I'm guilty of this fundamental doubt. It doesn't seem to matter how often God has met my needs…the "what ifs" of the future always seem to demand more of my attention than my faith in God's promises. Why is it that when faced with a difficult stretch of road ahead, we have such a hard time remembering all those instances in the past when God has provided? I suppose part of the answer rests in the sinfulness of mankind. Perhaps too it has a little to do with pride. Most of us want to believe that the things we have in this life are the result of our own efforts. We work hard, we earn a living and it's because of that hard work that we can provide for ourselves and our families. If we're successful, we want to believe that it has everything to do with us, and very little to do with God. That illusion of self-sufficiency, however, can distort our relationship with God. The reality of life is that all that we have, all that we will ever have on this earth, comes from God. Both Old and New Testaments make this point crystal clear. King David, in one of his psalms, says it beautifully. "The eyes of all look to You, and You give them their food at the proper time. You open your hand and satisfy the desires of every living thing (Psalm 145:15-16). In the New Testament, James reiterates this fact. "Every good and perfect gift is from above, coming down from the Father of the heavenly lights, who does not change like shifting shadows (James 1: 17). My question to you is this…would you rather go this road alone, relying on your own strength and effort to meet your needs? Or are you willing to believe that your loving Father wants to shoulder your burdens and provide for everything you could possibly need in this life?

I learned a valuable lesson regarding this from some backyard birds one day. When the cold weather comes around, I put up my bird feeder and stock up on seed. One of my daily joys is caring for God's winged friends, and I love watching them congregate excitedly around the feeder after I fill it each morning. It has gotten to the point that most of my avian neighbors are perched expectantly in the trees when the back door opens, waiting for me to dole out breakfast. There are mainly sparrows with an occasional cardinal, blue jay, chickadee, nuthatch or robin. But my favorite of all the birds has to be the mourning dove. There is just something special about those doves. One day as I was looking out my window, I saw the usual assortments of visitors. Off about twenty feet from the feeder was a solitary dove. There were other doves there at the feeder, but this particular dove was all by herself. I watched and

Hope for Provision

waited for her to join the others, but she didn't. She just stayed by herself and watched everyone else eat. This bothered me because feeding the birds usually makes me happy. I like to feel that I've done my part to care for God's creatures. Why wasn't she willing to enjoy what I wanted to give her? I thought about it for a moment and then it dawned on me how much like that dove I often am with God. How often does God want to provide for me, but I sulk in a corner wondering where He is or why He hasn't helped me yet. The provision is there but for my own blindness I can't see it. Or worse yet, I look at what I think God has provided for everyone else, and it looks like He is more generous with others than He is with me. Then I feel a bit sheepish realizing that because of my sinful nature, I really don't deserve all that much from God to begin with. Thankfully, the grace of God extends to both person and bird alike. After a bit I checked back out the window, and there she was, with her other dove friends enjoying the seed at the feeder. What joy to see her there, and what joy we as children of God give our heavenly Father when we humbly and gratefully accept His gifts!

There are times when provision comes only after a surrender of our will to God's will. I have found in my own life that periods of drought often come when it seems I have gone off the path God has laid out for me. When the cares and concerns of this world have caused me to take my eyes off God, and I try to handle all my needs through my own strength, I will undergo a time of shortage and testing. As distressing as that time may be, I believe it's God's way of gently redirecting me back to Him. I can recall one particular day after such a period of drought. I had finally come to the end of my rope. I had run out of trying to find solutions to the particular problem. Finances were running short and bills were running long, and I couldn't force a solution no matter how hard I tried. I was spiritually exhausted as well, and I remember lying in bed that night and finally saying to God, "I lay it all at Your feet." I'm handling things all wrong and I want You to be the main priority in my life. I didn't feel any particular sense of peace after releasing that burden to the Lord, but the following day it seemed like I received the best news that I had received in a very long while. I got word that I was due a tax refund where I usually had none, a long expected payment from work arrived and I received a package that I had been waiting for. I'm careful to point out that our sense of joy and peace should not be dependent upon the change in our external circumstances, but I took it as a gentle reminder that it was my own mindset that was the greatest obstacle to having the hope of God's provision.

So often when we think of the Lord performing miracles and having a direct hand in providing for people's needs, our thoughts focus on those long ago miracles from the Bible. Those miracles seem so much more spectacular than what we may experience in our daily lives, don't they? Yet little miracles are still miracles and are a welcome reminder that God is reliably acting on our behalf each and every day. If we can believe in a

Hope for Provision

God of infinite possibilities, then we can accept that answers to prayer may come in any shape or form that the Lord chooses. None of us can know how or when God may answer a sincere prayer for provision. But one thing is for sure. God is not limited when it comes to creativity!

Ultimately I think the problem we have with the provision of God is that we have a slightly different opinion about what constitutes provision than God does. Truth be told, a lot of us would like God to answer our prayers in one fell swoop. Rather than receiving what we need on a daily basis, a little at a time, we want God to respond in a way that guarantees a lifetime supply that we can see. Wouldn't it be nicer to have enough money in the bank to last the rest of our lives, rather than having to constantly ask God for what we need every day? While winning the lottery may seem like the answer to our prayers, God knows that how He responds to our needs may then determine how we respond to His calling. Proverbs 30 records the request of Agur to the Lord regarding this issue…"give me neither poverty nor riches, but give me only my daily bread. Otherwise I may have too much and disown you and say, 'Who is the Lord?' Or I may become poor and steal, and so dishonor the name of my God." (Proverbs 30: 8-9) If we look back at how God provided for the Israelites in the barren desert, it was one day at a time. In fact, God gave the people specific instructions to collect only enough manna for a day. Anything more and the extra would spoil. Before the Sabbath, they were to collect enough manna for two days, so that they could obey the Lord's command to not work on the Sabbath. Under those circumstances, the second days' supply did not spoil. Each time we pray the Lord's Prayer, we pray "give us this day our daily bread". Not monthly or yearly bread, but one day at a time. As hard as it can be to admit it, being in want from day to day keeps us closer to God and more in tune to our absolute need for Him. When times are good and supply is plentiful, it's easy to start feeling that we no longer need God. My question to you now is this…which will become your first priority, your immediate needs or your relationship with God? When your first priority is God, He usually makes sure that everything else falls into its proper place. If only we could more easily remember the words of Matthew 6:33, "But seek first His kingdom and His righteousness, and all these things will be given to you as well."

Chapter 4

HOPE FOR HEALING

O Lord my God, I cried out to You for help, and You restored my health.
Psalm 30: 2, NLT

My health may fail, and my spirit may grow weak, but God remains the strength of my heart; He is mine forever.
Psalm 73: 26, NLT

Perhaps one of the hardest things a person can face in this life is getting sick or hurt. In this busy world of ours, we might even consider it an inconvenience when the common cold sidelines us for a few days or we sprain an ankle playing basketball. There's just too much to do in the day to get sick, right? We tend to take for granted that medical advances and present day practices make life generally safer and healthier than what people had to deal with hundreds of years ago. While colds and mild muscle strains create temporary challenges to our hectic schedules, think for an instance what it would be like if they weren't temporary? What if sickness and chronic pain were a part of your everyday life? Or maybe you aren't the one affected by these struggles, but a loved one or friend is. The emotional pain from seeing someone else suffer can be significant. Regardless of who it may be, the physical consequences of disease or injury can dramatically affect and severely limit every aspect of life. While relationship issues or financial problems can weigh heavily on a person, it's likely you've heard someone say during times of trial, "At least you have your health". When that's no longer the case, however, the future can be a very uncertain and scary prospect…a future where it's hard to be hopeful for tomorrow. A diagnosis of cancer, multiple sclerosis, or rheumatoid arthritis can have you asking questions like "Is this what I'm going to have to live with for the rest of my life?", or even worse, "Will this disease eventually take my life?"

After a diagnosis of cancer or other serious illness, there's an understandable period of denial before the reality of the situation sinks in. You may desperately want to believe that the diagnosis was a mistake, or at the least, inaccurate. If that isn't the case, however, and the hard truth of the diagnosis remains, the inevitable question becomes "What now?" From a spiritual perspective, you probably have some questions you want answered. "Why did God let this happen to me?" "Can God heal me?" *Will* God heal me?" Often we are left with more questions than answers. We pray to God for healing, but in the midst of the pain and fear it can feel as if God isn't listening. Although it's tempting to believe that God may have turned His back on us, never doubt that God answers our prayers. In those periods of presumed silence, remember that God has not and will not abandon you.

It's human nature to want to know why bad things like illness happen to us. We want to understand what purpose is being served by God allowing this trial to come into our life. Somehow it seems easier to endure long pain filled days knowing that illness or injury isn't just some random occurrence. Why *would* God allow such suffering in a person's life?

There's certainly no shortage of individuals in the Bible who faced health issues. At times there was some inkling as to why the illness and injury occurred. In other instances, no real reason for the trouble was made known. Sometimes it was clear that God used illness to test a person's faith. There were other instances where illness occurred not because of any wrongdoing on a person's part, but because God wanted to demonstrate his power and mercy. Other times He wanted to teach someone to rely on Him more. Still other times it seemed that God used illness to get a person's attention and direct that person back into His will.

If living a righteous and God-pleasing life could protect a person from illness, then no one should have been safer than Job, right? He was one of those individuals in the Bible who was a charter member of the "Righteousness Hall of Fame". In fact, in the first chapter of the Old Testament book named after this well-respected man, Job was described as "blameless and upright; he feared God and shunned evil." (Job 1:1) So why did

The God of Hope

God allow such a righteous man as Job to be struck down with a skin disease so painful that he wished he had never been born? Does God allow such suffering to test the faith of His children? It would seem that sometimes He does. In the first chapters of Job, the Lord and Satan are engaged in a battle over Job and the reason for his righteous living. Satan argues that Job is only devoted to the Lord because God protects him from danger. In response, God allows Satan to destroy all Job's children and take his possessions from him. After such a tremendous loss, no one could fault Job if he blamed God for his misfortune. But Job doesn't turn away from God. Satan now tries to convince God that the only reason Job has remained faithful is that his health has been protected. "A man will give all he has for his own life. But stretch out Your hand and strike his flesh and bones, and he will surely curse You to Your face." (Job 2: 4-5) As a means of testing this theory, God allows Job to be afflicted with painful sores all over his body. There wasn't anything that Job had done to deserve this affliction, yet it came into his life as a test of his faith. Even Job's wife questioned why her husband remained faithful to God. "Are you still holding on to your integrity? Curse God and die!" (Job 2: 9) What was Job's response to her? "Shall we accept good from God, and not trouble?" (Job 2: 10) Even in the midst of the suffering he held steadfast to the Lord. I pray that none of us would have to go through what Job suffered, but if that be God's will for our lives, may we be found as faithful as Job in the midst of our pain.

Hope for Healing

When faced with illness, we may have a tendency to believe that the disease or disability came as a result of our shortcomings, or as some sort of punishment from God. If you have ever felt this way, you're in good company. The disciples themselves had this mindset. In the tenth chapter of Mark, Jesus and His disciples met a man who had been blind since birth. The disciples questioned Jesus about the origin of the blindness. "Rabbi, who sinned, this man or his parents, that he was born blind?" (Mark 10: 2) To their understanding, the blindness had to be the result of a wrong done by someone in this family. Jesus set them straight on the matter. What was His reply? "Neither this man nor his parents sinned...but this happened so that the work of God might be displayed in his life."(Mark 10: 3)

Could it be that God is waiting for us to pray to Him for healing? Certainly we know that God has the authority and power to heal us if He so chooses. Does He sometimes hold off on healing because He is waiting for us to approach Him with our medical needs? In the book of second Chronicles, King Asa was faced with a debilitating illness. The Bible simply describes his condition as a disease in his feet. What stands out about his illness, however, was Asa's response to the illness. "Though his disease was severe, even in his illness he did not seek help from the Lord, but only from the physicians." (2 Chronicles 16: 12) Let me be perfectly clear here. I'm in no way advocating that we not take advantage of the resources which modern medicine has to offer. God certainly has provided doctors and hospitals and modern medical technology for the good of society and we are blessed to have them. What I'm pointing out, though, is that we should look to the Great Physician first for our healing. He shouldn't be our last resort, when all other medical treatments have failed or fallen short. Depending on the Lord for healing is critical for both our physical and spiritual health. Don't leave God out of the healing process. Whatever affliction you may be suffering from, God wants to be the one you turn to for strength, solace and physical renewal.

Are there actually times when God may use physical illness and/or disability to get our attention; to steer us back onto the straight and narrow path, so to speak? It would seem so, based on examples from both the Old and New Testaments. Moses' own sister, Miriam, experienced this firsthand. She and her brother Aaron had begun grumbling against Moses…possibly a bit of sibling jealousy involved. She and Aaron had been complaining about Moses' foreign wife. The two siblings also began to think that they could do as good a job as their brother in leading the Israelite nation. The Lord disagreed and in response struck Miriam with leprosy, an incurable skin disease. Realizing his and his sister's sin, Aaron pleaded with Moses to forgive them of their foolishness. Moses prayed to the Lord on his sister's behalf and the Lord healed Miriam, but only after exiling her outside the Israelite camp for seven days (Numbers 12).

Hope for Healing

The Israelite nation as a whole felt the effects of their disobedience in the desert. Once again the Jewish people had become impatient with God and were complaining about their situation. In response, God sent poisonous snakes among them. Many people were bitten by the snakes and died. When the people realized they had sinned against God, they approached Moses and repented, "We sinned when we spoke against the Lord and against you. Pray that the Lord will take the snakes away from us." (Numbers 21: 7) Moses prayed on behalf of the Israelites, and the Lord instructed him to fashion a bronze snake on a pole…everyone who was bitten and looked at that snake survived. After that close call, I'll bet the Israelites who survived never looked at a snake the same way again.

Saul was on the road to Damascus when he was struck blind by God. Saul had spent many years zealously persecuting the early Christians. In fact he was on his way to Damascus to take any Christians he found there back to Jerusalem as prisoners. God used sudden blindness to get Saul's attention. In a profound reversal of attitude, Saul was converted to a disciple of Christ, and after three days God restored his sight (Acts 9). After that life changing encounter, this man who became known as St. Paul spent the rest of his life spreading the good news of the Gospel wherever he traveled.

I want to again reiterate that I'm by no means suggesting that a person's illness or physical affliction is the direct result of their sin. Far from it, there are many godly men and women who are suffering infirmities despite their living a God-pleasing life. That reality along with not knowing why you're suffering may be the hardest burden to bear. Wanting to know why something is happening to us is an understandable part of the process, but we must not let the question of why overshadow God's sovereignty and control of our situation. The truth is we may never know in this lifetime why God has allowed something like illness to afflict us. Despite the unanswered questions, however, we must never forget that whatever suffering we may be going through, God is with us.

As much as we would like to know the answer to why God allows physical suffering into our lives, another important question each of us needs to consider is "Can God heal?" Right now, do you in your heart believe that God is capable of healing you, no matter what you may be facing? Certainly, there are plenty of examples of modern day medical miracles. God, in His sovereignty, appears quite capable of healing even the most incurable diseases man has to face in this day and age. But do *you* believe that God can actually bring you healing?

If you can accept that God is capable of healing, the next question becomes *"Will* He heal me?" Certainly a loving and merciful God would want to heal His children when they cry out to Him, right? But what happens if there is no quick answer to that question, or even worse, God's answer is no? That's where our earthly and eternal perspectives can sometimes get all mixed up. So often we think only of our life here on earth and the future that we can envision. If we're suffering, we want to be healed quickly. If we're in pain, we want the pain to end. That's another very real part of human nature. After all, what good can possibly come out of suffering? What potential lesson could God be trying to teach us through all the pain? Would you for a moment be willing to entertain that it might be our very suffering that opens up the line of communication with and dependency on God? That what we suffer through today helps to bridge the temporary of this life to what will be the hope filled existence of our eternal life? Will God heal you in your earthly lifetime? The answer may be yes. It may be yes, but not right away. Or it may be no. Whatever the answer that God gives, you can be sure that His answer is given to ensure that your perfect heavenly body will be present with Him in eternity.

King Hezekiah was one of the many kings of Judah. Although Hezekiah was a godly ruler, God still allowed a serious illness to plague him. At the point of death, Hezekiah was visited by the prophet Isaiah, who told him, "This is what the Lord says: Put your house in order, because you are going to die: you will not recover." (2 Kings 20:1) Now if a great prophet like Isaiah said that to you, that wouldn't leave much room for hope, would it? There isn't much wiggle room to be had there. "You are going to die"...that's about as blunt a statement as can be made. What's amazing about this event is that despite the perceived hopelessness of the situation, there *was* still hope for Hezekiah. It would appear that God had made up His mind about

The God of Hope

Hezekiah's fate. God isn't one who usually changes His mind…His words are often set in stone. Yet look what happened to Hezekiah next. The Bible says that "Hezekiah turned his face to the wall and prayed to the Lord, 'Remember, O Lord, how I have walked before you faithfully and with wholehearted devotion and have done what is good in your eyes.' And Hezekiah wept bitterly. Before Isaiah had left the middle court, the word of the Lord came to him: 'Go back and tell Hezekiah, the leader of My people, 'This is what the Lord, the God of your father David, says: I have heard your prayer and seen your tears; I will heal you. On the third day from now you will go up to the temple of the Lord. I will add fifteen years to your life.'" (2 Kings 20: 2-6)

Despite God's statement that he would be healed, King Hezekiah was still human. He had some doubts. He asked Isaiah for a sign that God would indeed heal him. Ever patient with His children, God made the shadow of the sun go backward on the stairway of Ahaz to prove that what He said was true. In a seemingly hopeless situation, God heard the desperate cries of one of His own. Did Hezekiah deserve to be healed? Perhaps not. What do you think caused God to change His mind about Hezekiah? Was it the king's claims of lifelong devotion and service to the Lord, or was it his fervent prayers and tears? I tend to believe that the heartfelt supplications of a desperate man were what moved God the most. So take heart, beloved child of God! Despite the fear and uncertainty of illness that may be

Hope for Healing

facing you or a loved one, we all remain in the embrace of our merciful Lord. He hears our prayers and sees our tears, and He can move heaven and earth on our behalf. No situation is hopeless when we are resting firmly in the palm of God's hand!

Jairus, a ruler in the Jewish synagogue, knew the pain of a dying child. His only daughter lay close to death, and she was only twelve years old. This desperate father fell at Jesus' feet, begging Him to come to his house. Before Jesus could go, someone from the house arrived and gave Jairus the news he was dreading…his daughter was dead. Jesus reassured this grieving father. "Don't be afraid, just believe, and she will be healed." (Luke 8: 30) Jesus went to Jairus' house and proceeded to bring this child back to life. Jesus had returned the life of this precious child to her parents.

The widow of Zarephath had seen more than her fair share of trouble and heartache. As a widow, she was considered one of the lowliest in society, and because of her status, life for her and her son was very difficult. In the previous chapter we saw how God had used the prophet Elijah to provide for this small family's needs. Anyone might consider that this was enough hardship for this poor woman to endure. Yet it seemed that after that crisis was resolved, another one took its place. The son of this poor widow took ill. His condition grew progressively worse, until finally he stopped breathing. His mother, beaten down and beleaguered, confronted Elijah. "What do you have against me, O man of God? Did you come to remind me of my

The God of Hope

sin and kill my son?" (1 Kings 17: 18) Have you ever felt like this woman? Do you look at your illness or affliction as some sort of punishment from God? Do you feel that God has perhaps unjustly targeted you or someone you love, and you honestly don't know why?

I imagine Elijah could understand this woman's response, especially after all she and her son had been through. What could he do to address this widow's questions and heartache? Elijah's response, as ours should be, is to turn to the outstretched arms of the Lord. Elijah took the boy in his arms and carried him to his bed. He then cried out to the Lord. "O Lord my God, have you brought tragedy also upon the woman I am staying with by causing her son to die?" (1 Kings 17: 20) Then Elijah stretched himself out on the boy three times and cried to the Lord, "O Lord my God, let this boy's life return to him!" (1 Kings 17: 21) God heard Elijah's prayer and brought the child back to life. When Elijah carried the boy, now alive, back to his mother, her response was this…"Now I know that you are a man of God and that the word of the Lord from your mouth is the truth." (1 Kings 17: 24) If she had had any doubts about God's sovereignty and grace before, this act of healing certainly must have reassured her of His love and mercy.

In 2008, Rae Kupferschmidt, a sixty-five year old wife and mother living in Minnesota, suffered a massive cerebral hemorrhage that left her clinically brain dead. The doctors gave her no hope for recovery, much less survival. Faced with such devastating news, her family followed her last wishes, removed her from life support, brought her home from the hospital and began making funeral arrangements. Less than three hours home from the hospital, Rae began to awaken. Her daughter, a surgical technician, at first thought it was a temporary moment of consciousness before death. As time went on, however, Rae continued to improve. Soon after that she was in physical therapy, with doctors extending the possibility of a full recovery. To Rae and her family, there is no doubt that God was instrumental in this modern day miracle. Rae's husband, Alan, knew the source of his wife's healing. "We have been blessed and blessed and blessed", he told reporters. Rae put it another way. "God's got something for me to do. When I learn it, I'll unfold it and follow it." Having been through what seemed to be a terminal illness, Rae emerged physically renewed. Even more importantly, her spiritual health was alive and well. Yes, God *can* heal in remarkable ways!

If you tend to be of a skeptical nature, as I often am, you may have a hard time reconciling the miracles of the Bible with anything miraculous that might happen in the present day. While we may become hardened by the pain of disease and death that pervades everyday life, we must never become blind to God's hand of healing that still works in our lives and the lives of those around us. Sometimes miracles are right in front of us…we just need to recognize them when they happen. Certainly Rae Kupferschmidt and her family would say they experienced a modern day miracle. Have you ever heard of a cancer patient that goes to his doctor for a recheck and finds that his cancer is no longer present? Or how about the person whose heart stops and has been legally dead for more minutes than modern medicine says it's possible to recover from? Yet they recover, with no permanent health effects. Oftentimes when these recoveries occur, we tend to regard them as miracles of modern science and medicine, not miracles of God. Perhaps though, we should look at them as God's miracles that might utilize the resources of modern day medicine. In the bigger picture, it is God alone who is the ultimate determiner of life and death.

Nowhere may this theme have been more evident than in the relatively recent case of Dr. Kent Brantly and his miraculous recovery from a deadly disease. Can you recall the Ebola virus crisis that occurred a few years back? If so you might remember hearing about Dr. Brantly, a physician working in Africa with the medical mission team from Samaritan's Purse. Kent felt called to minister to the people of Africa even before Ebola had become an epidemic within the country. When the virus began spreading, Kent remained in Liberia to treat those victims who had been infected. Of the many cases he had been involved with, only one patient had survived, so he knew full well the implications of contracting the virus. Despite taking the best medical precautions that were available to Kent and his team, he and another staff member, Nancy Writebol, were infected with the virus. Over the course of several days, both their conditions deteriorated significantly. This virus was relentless in claiming the lives of those it affected, and the impending deaths of these two individuals, who only wanted to serve God, seemed imminent. In what can only be regarded as providential divine intervention, there came word that a new drug existed which had shown remarkable promise in Ebola-infected monkeys. The problem was that this drug, consisting of Ebola fighting antibodies known as ZMapp, had never been tested in humans. Unbelievably, one course of this drug treatment was actually in the Sierra Leone, and was transported to where Brantly and Writebol were hospitalized. Unfortunately, there were two patients and only enough drug for one individual. The treatment consisted of three doses, and they were not to be split up between patients, as this would seriously compromise the treatment's effectiveness. The doctor in charge of decision-making, Dr. Lance Plyler, was also friends with both victims. How would he decide who to give the drug to? What now? The drug had to be thawed first, and Dr. Plyler made the decision to give the treatment to Nancy Writebol. While the drug was thawing, however, Dr. Brantly's condition deteriorated even further, and his friend recognized that death was fast approaching. Dr. Plyler agonized over what to do next. He chose the best option he could think of. He prayed, and asked all those he could contact to pray for his friends. Then Dr. Plyler, when recounting the chain of events, described a sense of calm that came over him, and knew what he had to do. He made the decision to split the treatment doses and administer the drug to *both* Brantly and Writebol. Within hours of receiving their doses, both patients' conditions improved dramatically. Their rapid clinical improvement was considered nothing short of amazing. After being flown stateside to Emory University for further treatment, both Kent and Nancy fully recovered. The availability of this experimental drug is certainly a breakthrough in modern medicine, but the timing and sequence of events most certainly had the fingerprint of God stamped on this miracle. Throughout his ordeal, Dr. Brantly remained focused on the fact that, despite whatever might happen, he was in the hands of his loving Father. His goal was to remain faithful to God despite an unknown future and to glorify Him regardless of the outcome. As a result of his life threatening illness, many people around the world were compelled to pray for him and his coworker, and his story most certainly exposed the world to the grace and mercy of a loving God. When Dr. Plyler was asked by others what he thought had saved his friend Kent's life, his answer was a quick and confident one. "I call it prayers and antibodies, in that order". Dr. Brantly's story is certainly a testament to Psalm 50: 15, "Call on me in the day of trouble; I will deliver you, and you will honor me."

    For every story of miraculous healing such as Dr. Brantly's, there are unfortunately others where healing does not come despite prolonged prayers and pleading to God. That's why it can be so difficult to understand why God may choose not to heal a person right away. What if God chooses to allow a person to suffer through a protracted period of illness, or worse, does not heal the person at all? From our vantage point, that can be the worst. Because none of us can see into the future, how can a person know if the ultimate intent of God is to bring healing, albeit delayed, versus no healing at all? It's during these uncertain times that our faith can be tested the most. How easy it can be to doubt God's love when we acknowledge that He can heal us and yet seems unwilling to do so.

The New Testament describes a woman who had suffered from bleeding for twelve years. The Bible doesn't say exactly what type of bleeding this woman suffered from, but it had gone on long enough and was severe enough that she had "suffered a great deal under the care of many doctors and had spent all she had, yet instead of getting better she grew worse." (Mark 5: 26) Anyone who has suffered from blood loss severe enough to cause anemia knows how exhausted it can make you feel. Combine that with the frustration of not getting any relief from medical treatment and the depletion of her savings, and I imagine this poor woman had very little hope left. No hope except for Jesus, that is. When she heard about this man who could heal the sick, she just had to meet Him. She snuck up behind Him while He was surrounded by a crowd and touched His clothes. That one touch brought her healing that no one else could bring her in twelve long years. For as long as she had been made to suffer with her illness, I'm sure that the healing she received from that one touch of the Son of God changed her whole spiritual outlook on life. She had met the Great Physician and her life would never be the same!

If twelve years seem like a long time to suffer from an illness, how long would thirty-eight years seem to be? Such was the case for one man in Jerusalem. We don't know exactly what was wrong with this person other than being described as an invalid in the book of John. He and a number of other disabled individuals spent their time in the city near a pool called Bethesda. They all hoped to be healed from the waters of the pool if they could reach the pool at the correct time. When Jesus meets this invalid who has suffered for almost four decades, He asks the man a seemingly blunt question. "Do you want to get well?" I wonder what might have been going through that man's mind when he heard Jesus' question. Of course he wanted to get well, right? "'Sir", the invalid replied, "I have no one to help me into the pool when the water is stirred. While I am trying to get in, someone else goes down ahead of me.'"(John 5: 7) Can you for a moment put yourself in this man's shoes? Imagine that you're left alone, unable to get yourself into that pool of healing waters and that no one is willing to offer you any help. Not only would you have to deal with the burden of your infirmity, but I think it would be hard not to be bitter about the lack of help…especially when you see other people being healed because they reach the waters ahead of you. That would be a lot for any person to have to contend with for that long a period of time. In the end, this man didn't need those healing waters because he had found the One who was the true source of "living water." Jesus spoke a few words to the man and at once he was healed.

Even so, the most difficult situation to accept is when healing does not come at all. Perhaps the harshest reality of our earthly existence is that no one is immune to pain and sickness. Ultimately our life will end in physical death. Only a few individuals from Biblical times avoided a physical death and were brought directly to heaven, but I wouldn't count on that way as our escape from this world. Why does God heal certain people and not others? I suppose that alone could be the subject of its' own book. Why is it that good people are afflicted with horrible diseases, while people who have turned their backs on God seem to float through life physically unscathed? It certainly doesn't seem fair. How can a person feel hopeful in this life when every day is marked by more physical suffering? God could surely heal me or my loved one if He wanted to, so why doesn't He?" Unfortunately, we can go through this life and never find the answer to those questions. In those moments of despair, however, it is critical that we not give way to bitterness or anger. During those times of God's silence or seeming apathy, we need to cling tightly to Him rather than push Him away.

When healing doesn't come or there is no miraculous recovery, our very sense of hope can be shaken to the core. We often question God's love and sense of mercy, especially when

The God of Hope

those afflicted by illness are who we consider to be good people. Several years back the nation embraced the story of Randy Pausch and "The Last Lecture". On September 18, 2007, Randy, a computer science professor, gave a lecture at Carnegie Mellon University describing his battle with pancreatic cancer. For Randy, there was no recovery or miracle that spared his life. He died less than a year after giving that lecture. Yet he faced the uncertainty of his earthly future with dignity, strength, humility and humor. I don't know if he was a religious man, but I do know that that were many people praying for God to heal him. I was one of those people, and I was truthfully very upset with God when I first heard of Randy's death. Why would God let someone like Randy, someone so inspiring to those around him, die like that? It just seemed so unfair. He had a wife and young children who depended on him. Reflecting back on the course of his illness, it was apparent that this man generously opened himself up to people he had never even met. He became a source of inspiration to everyone who was present at his last lecture, and to those who may have read about him or seen him on TV. He used his last days on earth to provide hope to those in a similar situation. He never demonstrated any bitterness as a result of his situation, and never fostered an attitude of "Why me?" He accepted what had befallen him and tried to make the best of the situation. That may have been of little consolation to his family, but his advice to cherish the days that you have on this earth with those you love, truly found an audience. His suffering may have given someone else the roadmap to get them through their own personal trial of illness. Some of you may disagree with Randy's story pointing to a God who gives hope. Here was a good man with a family, who got a horrible disease and ultimately died well before he should have. That's certainly one way to look at it. But the truth is that we all die. Some of us will die at a ripe old age, having had minimal physical ailments. Others of us will die sooner than expected, and perhaps having suffered tremendously during our time on earth. But we all die…we all reach the end of our life. So the lesson about the hope that exists in this life is what you do with the time that you have while on this earth. Randy made good use of that time by the valuable lessons he taught the rest of us. Someone once said that when looking at a person's tombstone, the birth year and death year were not nearly as important as the dash in between the two. That's because the dash represents what a person did with their life…it's a measure of the fullness of that life. Can you say that the dash of your life will represent the best that you can offer to God?

Joni Eareckson Tada is a modern day example of someone who personifies hopefulness despite severe physical limitations. A diving accident as a teenager left Joni a quadriplegic. Despite her physical challenges, Joni has used her life as a witness to the grace and mercy of God. As an author and painter, she uses her talents to bring hope to all those around her. Her organization, "Joni and Friends" is a powerful force of ministry for the disabled community. Although physical healing has not come to her, she nonetheless uses her God given talents to advance the kingdom of God. Rather than harboring bitterness or being overcome by despair, Joni has used her experience to be a beacon of light to the world, describing freely the generosity of God's grace, and teaching that spiritual health is ultimately so much more important than physical health. Her quadriplegia has contributed to her work in God's kingdom in a greater way than perhaps if she were still able to walk. Often times, it is during times of physical illness and infirmity that we learn to more heavily rely on God to carry us through. Self-sufficiency may be the lesson of the world, but God may use various means to get us to understand and accept our need for dependency on Him. In the end, learning to rely on God for our help and our future is a much better way to go than relying on ourselves.

If you've ever watched the TV sitcom "The Middle", you've probably seen the actor who portrays the youngest child Brick. That actor, Atticus Shaffer, is a young man of faith who has overcome physical obstacles and is quite an inspiration in his own right. Atticus suffers from a genetic condition known as osteogenesis imperfecta, a disease that results in his bones being fragile. As a result, his body is more prone to fractures than someone not affected by the condition. Rather than let this disease define and limit him, this young man has achieved an impressive level of success while serving as a role model to those around him. He doesn't harbor bitterness but is instead thankful to God for the life he lives in spite of the physical challenges. Acknowledging God's many blessings to him, he in turn wants to bless others by encouraging them to fulfill God given dreams.

Individuals like Joni Erickson Tada and Atticus Shaffer have learned that despite the challenges of their physical situations, there is reassurance in the fact that God is present in their lives. He sees what they are going through on a daily basis and He provides the strength through which they can press onward in their walk of faith. The apostle Paul clarifies what it means to look to the Lord in spite of one's afflictions. In second Corinthians Paul describes a "thorn in the flesh" that was given to him in order not to become conceited from the profound revelations that God had shown to him. The Bible doesn't explain what that thorn was, but it was something severe enough to cause Paul tremendous suffering. Three times Paul pleaded with the Lord to remove the thorn from him, but the Lord's response to him was, "My grace is sufficient for you, for My power is made perfect in weakness." Paul could have been resentful about the Lord's answer. He could have even decided that he was no longer going to work for the Lord. Instead, this is how he responded to the negative answer from God…"Therefore I will boast all the more gladly about my weaknesses, so that Christ's power may rest on me. That is why, for Christ's sake, I delight in weaknesses, in insults, in hardships, in persecutions, in difficulties. For when I am weak, then I am strong." (2

The God of Hope

Corinthians 12: 9-10) Paul understood that this thorn in the flesh resulted in greater dependence on God. When the day was long and the pain was overwhelming, God would be there for Paul and would carry him when this apostle had no strength left of his own. For all those enduring seemingly endless physical suffering, remember that God's grace and strength are available to you. God will never forsake you, no matter how great the pain. And one day, when you stand face to face with Him in heaven, there will be no more pain, no more illness, no more suffering. That's a wonderful reason for hope today!

As someone who spends a fair bit of time around animals, I'm continually amazed at their ability to deal with illness and physical limitations. Where once such physical burdens may have resulted in their premature death, advanced veterinary care has allowed animals to live longer and fuller lives. I guess where we differ from animals is that most times they don't know or consciously appreciate their limitations. Anyone who has had a dog or cat who rebounds quickly after major surgery or who has witnessed a paraplegic dog scooting around in a custom cart appreciates the resiliency of animals. Sometimes I think they may even have a great advantage over their human counterparts. Where we tend to dwell on our illnesses and physical shortcomings, they don't give it much thought. Where we worry and agonize over illness and injury, they live life as if their limitations are of no consequence. I had a cat who I loved dearly. After I had adopted him, I found out that

Hope for Healing

he had an incurable immunodeficiency disease. I knew that this disease could potentially shorten his life span and leave him susceptible to a number of life threatening illnesses. In truth, for the nine years that God blessed me with him, there wasn't a day that went by where I didn't worry about that reality. I was always on the lookout for the first signs that the immunodeficiency disease was getting ready to rear its ugly head. As for my cat, well, he couldn't have cared less that he had this disease. He lived a pretty contented life by all human standards. When his life finally came to a close, it was from something completely unrelated to that disease I had worried so much about. My cat taught me many valuable lessons during his life, but in this instance he reminded me that it is much better to focus on the blessings in life that God has daily provided, than to exhaust oneself worrying about what a diagnosis or illness may bring about in the distant future. For both humans and animals, it is reassuring to know that "In His hand is the life of every creature, and the breath of all mankind" (Job 12: 10).

    For most of this chapter, the focus has been on healing associated with physical ailments. While disease and injury can present significant challenges to our physical well-being, I don't want to minimize the challenges faced by those individuals who have suffered greatly because of emotional traumas in their lives. Emotional pain from past experiences can be every bit as debilitating and demoralizing as physical pain can be. Psychological and emotional abuse by family members and other influential people in a person's life can have devastating effects for years after the abuse. Scars from such abuse may not be physically visible, but their presence nonetheless can result in depression, withdrawal and other very real emotional consequences which can then lead to physical symptoms. Talk to a person who has suffered such abuse and often they will tell you that their emotional suffering allows them no relief. It is unrelenting and oftentimes paralyzing. While for these individuals there is no way to reverse the past and prevent the events that so dramatically changed their lives, the truth is that God is much more concerned with their present and future than with anything that has happened in the past. He can provide the strength and perseverance to overcome anything that may have left a person with deep emotional wounds. I love the sentiment presented in the fifth chapter of second Corinthians. "Therefore, if any man be in Christ, he is a new creature: old things are passed away; behold all things are become new" (2 Corinthians 5: 17 KJV). With Christ, you can start each day fresh, a clean slate, free of the painful memories of the past that may be holding you back. You have God's power to help you overcome. Embrace the truth of 2 Timothy 1: 7, "For God hath not given us the spirit of fear; but of power, and of love, and of a sound mind (KJV). Can you take Him at His word?

The truth is that in this life, you may never know the reason for your illness or injury. Whether you ever come to understand the purpose of physical or emotional suffering, you need to remember that God is sovereign, He is always with you, and He will never leave you even in the midst of that pain and suffering. You are safe in His arms and He has not forgotten you. He may choose to heal you and if He does remember to thank Him and praise Him. If for some reason physical or emotional healing is not God's will for your life, don't take this as a rejection from God. It doesn't mean that He has abandoned you or forsaken you. Although tempting to believe that that might be the case, God's eternal perspective on your situation transcends any glimpse of the horizon that you may be searching for. Your physical life is temporary…a fleeting moment when viewed through the lens of eternity. Your relationship with Him, however, is of greater worth than anything in this life you will have to endure. Yes, we will all die at some point, but physical death cannot snatch us from His loving arms if we will only embrace Him as our Father.

You may be familiar with an old saying that helps put the frailty of human existence into the proper perspective, especially in the midst of health struggles. The saying goes like this… "You don't have a soul. You are a soul. You have a body". At first glance, we may be a bit reluctant to consider that point of view. As earthly inhabitants, we tend to focus on the here and now…what we can physically see and feel and experience. Our earthly body is something quite tangible. When we look in the mirror we see the physical manifestations of it. Our soul, for all intents and purposes, is a much more abstract concept. When we look into that same mirror, it isn't our soul that we see looking back at us. Our reflection in the mirror shows the physical effects of aging, stress and disease. That only cements in our minds the perception that we are first and foremost body with soul…not the other way around. But if we were to look at our lives through the proper eternal lens, we would see with much clearer focus. Our momentary trials are achieving for us an eternal life with God, where we will be free from all disease, pain and trouble. We don't know for sure the bodily form we will have in heaven, but the essence of who we are spiritually, our soul, will be the foundation of our eternal existence. St. Paul describes it this way in the New Testament. "The body that is sown is perishable, it is raised imperishable; it is sown in dishonor, it is raised in glory; it is sown in weakness, it is raised in power; it is sown a natural body, it is raised a spiritual body" (1 Corinthians 15: 42-44). No matter the physical or emotional burdens you are facing right now, they will not last forever. God may choose to heal you in this earthly life, to ease your pain and suffering. Or for reasons known only to Him, He may choose to allow that suffering to continue in your life. Should the latter be the case, remember that one day you will exchange your worn out physical body for a perfect eternal one…one that will never know the physical limitations of this earthly life. Now that is most certainly a reason for hope!

Chapter 5

HOPE FOR FORGIVENESS

And what a difference between our sin and God's generous gift of forgiveness. For this one man, Adam, brought death to many through his sin. But this other man, Jesus Christ, brought forgiveness to many through God's bountiful gift.
Romans 5: 15, NLT

In Him we have redemption through His blood, the forgiveness of sins, in accordance with the riches of God's grace
Ephesians 1: 7

Have you ever been at a point in your life where you felt you had messed up so badly that God would surely want nothing to do with you? Have you ever felt that as far as God was concerned, you were past the point of no return? In your mind you had committed such a grievous sin or multitude of sins that there really was no hope of a fresh start? If you currently feel that you are a lost cause because of what fills up your yesterdays, then you need to take another look at your life. Be reassured of this fact...your tomorrows need not be dictated by what has happened in your past. If you feel that there's no hope for the future because of the mistakes you've made in the past, then this chapter is especially for you. God has an infinite capacity to take the broken and flawed parts of our lives and use our past experiences to mold us into someone new…someone who has unlimited potential for doing His work in this world.

Take a moment to look back on your life and try to think of the worst sin you've committed. Maybe you don't have to think for long because there's a memory that plagues each day with shame and regret. Maybe it was something that was done in the innocence and ignorance of youth, or perhaps it's an ongoing battle with an addiction that doesn't want to loosen its grip on you. What is there in your life that just won't allow you a peaceful nights' sleep and that weighs heavy on your heart? Everyone is guilty of some mistake or sin they wish had never happened. None of us can claim perfection, for we're all fatally flawed. Can you remember when you were a kid playing with your friends, and you called for a "do-over"? Have you ever wished for a "do-over" from your past so you could wipe the slate clean? The regret and self-condemnation from shouldering past sins has you believing you can be of absolutely no value to God. While you may be asking yourself how God can possibly use you after the things you've done, you need to remember that it's God who has the final say in what His future plans are for you. Don't let self-condemnation steal the joy and fulfillment from the life that God wants you to have.

An important question to ask yourself is "Where is this condemnation coming from?" Maybe you feel that it comes from

Hope for Forgiveness

God. Do you picture God as a stern disciplinarian who is just waiting to crack you over the head whenever you make a mistake? Perhaps you feel there's no way that God can forgive you for whatever you may have done in the past. Or can it be that you *do* believe God can forgive you, but you just can't forgive yourself? If that's the case, then you're dealing with guilt that the devil loves to use. What better way to make a potential servant of God ineffective than by overwhelming that person with false guilt...guilt that God never intended to be a part of your life?

In the contemporary Christian song, "Hello My Name Is", singer Matthew West describes the self-condemnation we can experience and the challenge it creates in our walk with God. The first verse of this song describes the nagging voice of regret that never lets us forget our shortcomings and the shame of past mistakes. The second verse highlights the power of defeat in life, where the burden of all that shame weighs so heavily on us that it keeps us from making a fresh start. In the end we give up hope and stop trying for a better life. In the face of regret and defeat, the greatest challenge is actually believing that no sin in our lives, whether past, present or future, is unforgiveable by God if we are willing to repent of it. Admittedly, acknowledging forgiveness in your head is not always the same as embracing it in your heart. The weight of perceived unforgiveness can feel like a millstone around your neck. You ask yourself, "How can I live a life for God when I have failed Him so badly?" If you've spoken these or similar words to yourself then please take heart. You're in good company! Despite your sins and shortcomings, there's a reason to hope. In fact, there's reason to rejoice! Who knows fully the wonderful plans for your life and all the great things you can do? God, of course! And He wants to change the world (or your corner of it) with your help!

If you still doubt your awesome potential in God's eyes, you need to take an encouraging look at the lives of some of the great Biblical heroes. The Bible is full of individuals who, despite failing God, received the full measure of His forgiveness. They were people who committed some serious sins, but were nonetheless used by God to carry out His plans. I'm always a little amazed when I read about how the Bible describes these heroes of faith, especially after seeing some of the things they did to disappoint God. I suppose that when I read their stories, I'm a harsher judge than God is. And that's exactly my point. We, as flawed humans, are often more critical of our fellow man than God is. Where we would be ready to write someone off, God envisions a future for them that is filled with hope.

When you get right down to it, it didn't take long in the Bible for the first sin to occur. Adam and Eve started out okay, but they made quick work out of being deceived by the devil. In fact, by the third chapter of Genesis, the very first book of the Bible, the serpent had convinced them that they could be like God, and they didn't put up much of a fight. That act of disobedience cost them their residence in the Garden of Eden.

Hope for Forgiveness

Despite their obvious disobedience, God showed the two of them mercy. He could easily have decided that His first human endeavor was a mistake, wiped the slate clean, and tried for Adam and Eve 2.0. Instead, He let them live, although they had to live out the rest of their lives facing the consequences of their sin. Of course, God knew that Adam and Eve's sin would lay the groundwork for His plan of eternal salvation through His Son.

If we jump to the next generation, we're introduced to Cain and Abel, the sons of Adam and Eve. By the fourth chapter of Genesis, the first murder has already been committed. Cain killed his brother Abel because he was angry that Abel had given a better offering to God than he had. As if murder wasn't bad enough, Cain made it worse by lying to God about it. The Bible makes it clear that Abel was an innocent victim and that Cain deserved punishment. God certainly had every right to end Cain's life at this point. But He didn't. Instead He spared Cain's life and even put a mark on him so that others wouldn't kill him for what he had done.

Abraham, the father of many nations, became too impatient to wait for the heir that God had promised him. Instead, he took matters into his own hands and slept with his wife's servant to get an heir. God forgave him and blessed him with another son, Isaac, who *was* the fulfillment of that promise. Isaac's son, Jacob, conspired with his mother to steal his older brother Esau's birthright. He lied to his father and was pretty devious about it. He still became the father of the twelve tribes

The God of Hope

of Israel. Moses was guilty of murder. Saved as a baby from Pharaoh's harmful intent, he was raised as an Egyptian royal. One day he saw an Egyptian beating a Hebrew slave, and in anger he killed the Egyptian. With this murderer, God led the entire Israelite nation out of Egypt. As for the Israelites, how many times did God forgive them? They had barely gotten out of Egypt before they started complaining about how hard the exodus was. If that wasn't bad enough, they began worshiping Baal and other false idols, even after everything God had done for them. It seemed they were on a perpetual roller coaster ride of sinning against God and being justifiably punished for it, then returning to Him, only to begin the whole cycle of disobedience again. At any time God could have said, "You know what…that's it. I've had enough" and destroyed the whole nation. But He didn't. Time and again He forgave them. There was always a second chance, and eventually they did reach that land flowing with milk and honey. It wasn't because of their goodness, but because of God's infinite grace and forgiveness!

When I think of a biblical figure that was highly regarded despite his shortcomings, my mind immediately jumps to King David. To me it's incredible that David was regarded as one of the great heroes of the Bible. He was the ancestor of our Savior, and considered to be one of the greatest kings of Israel. But when you look at his life, he made some seriously big mistakes. Even worse, some of his most grievous offenses weren't innocent mistakes at all. They were pretty cold and calculating in nature.

Let's start with a few of David's lesser sins. While David was king, he made the decision to bring the Ark of the Covenant back to Jerusalem. The ark was sacred and God had clearly defined how it was to be transported, and who was allowed to carry it. The only acceptable means of transporting the ark was to have the Levite priests carry it with poles. For whatever reason, David didn't obey God's instructions. Instead, David had the ark put on a cart that was pulled by oxen. When the oxen pulling the cart stumbled, one of the assistants put his hand on the ark to steady it. No one was allowed to touch the ark, and as a result, this man was immediately put to death by God. David was the one who had made the mistake, yet that man suffered the price for David's sin. On another occasion, David had instructed his military commander to take a census of the army. This may have seemed innocent enough, but what David was actually doing was bragging about how powerful a king he was. A census was only to be done at God's instruction, and God had not given the order. Because of this, God sent a message to David that he would have to suffer the consequences of his prideful behavior. David would have to choose between three years of famine, three months of being attacked by his nation's enemies, or three days of a plague. David settled on the plague, and countless people died because of his ego.

The God of Hope

Perhaps the best known example of David's sinfulness was that of his adulterous affair with Bathsheba. David committed a pretty blatant sin here when he decided he wanted another man's wife. The adultery was bad enough by itself, but it was the events around the actual sin that reflected a darker side of David's character. His slide down morality hill started when he chose to stay home while his army went off to battle. That left David with a little too much free time on his hands. Of course one thing led to another, and he eventually eyed the beautiful Bathsheba across the courtyard while she was bathing. He decides he has to have her for himself, but there's one catch. She's already married. At this point her marital status doesn't matter much to David, because after all he's king…and kings can have whatever they want. The end result is that he sleeps with her. Concerned that she might now be pregnant, he has her husband Uriah brought back from the battle front. David gets him drunk and tries to convince him to sleep with his wife while he's on furlough, so the timing of a baby wouldn't be so suspicious. Uriah, however, is an honorable man and he refuses. Uriah feels it's wrong to be spending time with his wife while his fellow soldiers are in harm's way. Now David is in a bit of a pickle. He's already in a hole but won't stop digging. His next step is to have Uriah sent back to duty and positioned on the front line of battle. Then the army commander is to have the rest of the troops withdraw. Of course this leaves Uriah alone like a sitting duck, and all but guarantees his death. Not only has David committed adultery, but he is now guilty of pre-meditated murder. Unlike Moses, who spontaneously murders someone in a fit of rage, David did a lot of planning to commit the perfect murder. Not until the prophet Nathan confronts him with his sin does David acknowledge it and pleads for forgiveness. God does forgive him, but because of his sin, he and Bathsheba lose that first child. I suppose if God had really wanted to judge David and Bathsheba harshly, He could have made Bathsheba barren from that point forward. Instead, David and Bathsheba go on to have a son named Solomon, who was widely regarded as the wisest king that Israel ever had.

When I think about David and all the sinful things he did in his life, I have to admit that I'm troubled that God could look so favorably on him. How could someone who did the things that David did be considered one of the greatest heroes of the Bible? I know he brought down Goliath and early on had a heart dedicated to God, but how could he fail God so miserably and yet go on to lead the life of faith that he did? Because our God is a loving and forgiving God! In fact, in the book of Acts, Paul describes David in these words…"He (God) testified concerning him, I have found David son of Jesse a man after My own heart; he will do everything I want him to do. From this man's descendants God has brought to Israel the Savior Jesus, as He promised." (Acts 13: 22-23) Those were pretty complimentary words for someone who had missed the mark more than once in his life. There was, of course, a price to be paid for David's sin, but God freely forgave him and a new chapter was begun in David's life. He received the clean slate that we all so desperately need and want. Then David was free to finish the work that God had in store for him. Offenses that we would consider game-enders are freely overlooked by God. This speaks volumes about how our God loves us, and how He is the generous provider of second chances. There's nothing that we have done or will do, that can separate us from His love. Nothing can keep us from being used by Him, if only we will repent and then accept His forgiveness.

Of all the kings that ruled Israel, King Ahab perhaps had the worst reputation. In fact, the Old Testament book of First Kings describes him this way…"There was never a man like Ahab, who sold himself to do evil in the eyes of the Lord." (1 Kings 21: 25) Besides practicing idolatry, Ahab and his wife Jezebel were responsible for persecuting the prophets of the Lord. Ahab had no moral center and did whatever he wanted to, with complete disregard for the laws of God. There happened to be a man named Naboth who owned a vineyard near the king's palace. Ahab wanted the vineyard for a vegetable garden, but Naboth wouldn't sell. This land was his family's inheritance and it meant more to him than money. Because Ahab's offer had been declined, Ahab and his wife hatched a scheme to get the land anyway. Jezebel cooked up a plot to slander Naboth and as a result he was stoned to death. After that, Ahab took possession of the vineyard. Because of the king's treachery, God sent the

Hope for Forgiveness

prophet Elijah to Ahab with a message of condemnation. Ahab was to die, and punishment for his wickedness would be carried out on his descendants. When Ahab, as evil as he was, heard the judgment against him, the Bible says "he tore his clothes, put on sackcloth and fasted. He lay in sackcloth and went around meekly."(1 Kings 21: 27) In other words, he humbled himself and showed remorse for what he had done. What then was God's response to this man who had defied Him so often? The Lord spoke these words to Elijah, "Have you noticed how Ahab has humbled himself before Me? Because he has humbled himself, I will not bring this disaster in his day, but I will bring it on his house in the days of his son." (1 Kings 21: 29) There would still be consequences for the evil that Ahab had committed in his lifetime, but God showed this man mercy in spite of his sins. If God can mercifully grant a man like Ahab forgiveness, he will certainly grant forgiveness to anyone with a contrite heart, no matter what they may have done in their life. God's grace is limitless!

Even those with a stubborn heart can be used by God, despite their reluctance to serve. A perfect case in point is that of the Old Testament rebel, Jonah. Jonah had been told by God to travel to the city of Nineveh, in order to preach to its inhabitants and turn that city from its wicked ways. Jonah, however, wanted no part of that action, so he headed off in the opposite direction. He boarded a ship bound for Tarshish, in order "to flee from the Lord." (Jonah 1:3). Jonah's actions were about as blatantly disobedient as any could be. His outward defiance of God's instructions would seem to deserve swift and harsh punishment. Yet God showed tremendous patience with Jonah, because He had plans for this wayward individual. But first He needed to get Jonah's attention. How did He get it? Well, He whipped up a furious storm that threatened everyone on board the ship Jonah was on. Eventually, the crew realized the storm was a result of Jonah being on board, and they wanted to know what to do, because they were afraid of the Lord. Jonah told them, "Pick me up and throw me into the sea and it will become calm. I know that it is my fault that this great storm has come upon you." (Jonah 1:12) At first the crew tried to find a different solution, but without success. So they threw Jonah overboard, and immediately the storm died down. From Jonah's disobedience, this crew came to learn firsthand of the Lord's sovereignty. What became of Jonah after he ended up in the ocean? God could have let him drown because of his disobedience. Instead, He sent a great fish to swallow Jonah up. For three days and three nights Jonah spent his time in the belly of that fish. How's that for getting a person's attention? I would imagine that Jonah had some serious moments of introspection while confined in those dark, smelly quarters. Then at God's command, that fish vomited Jonah onto dry land. When Jonah had recovered from his underwater exile, God's command to him was the same as before. He was to preach to the Ninevites, in order for them to turn from their wicked ways. Jonah still wasn't thrilled about

Hope for Forgiveness

God's instructions, and he certainly didn't become an instant fan of the Ninevites. But after his intimate encounter with a certain fish, he obeyed God this time. As a result, the Ninevites responded to his preaching, declared a fast and repented of their sins. Although Jonah had thumbed his nose at God and made a quick exit in order to circumvent God's plan, God still looked past all that and was determined to make use of a less than enthusiastic Jonah. If God can look past all that Jonah did, certainly He won't hold our sins against us if we'll submit to His will!

If we look to the New Testament for an example of a sinner who went on to do great things for the Lord, one has only to think of St. Paul. Paul was one of the great New Testament heroes. He didn't start out that way, however. In fact, Paul (or Saul as he was first called) was about as far from being a useful servant of God as you can get. He spent most of his time terrorizing the early Christians, and seemed to take pleasure in being an obstacle to the work of the Lord. In the book of Acts, Paul was right there when one of the early Christian workers, Stephen, was being stoned. The Bible states that the witnesses to the stoning laid their clothes at the feet of Saul. Acts 8:1 reports, "And Saul was there, giving approval to his (Stephen's) death." What hope could there be for someone like this? One would think that this man's future was a foregone conclusion. But on the road to Damascus, God revealed a different direction for Paul's life. What Paul had done in the past was irrelevant, because God had big plans for him. In reality, it was the past experiences of Paul's former life that propelled him to be the driving force for spreading God's word throughout the ancient world. Paul knew what horrible sins he had committed, and he was determined to live a life that would never take the forgiveness he had received for granted. He treasured his second chance, and was willing to suffer and sacrifice his life, if need be, to proclaim the hope that could only come from the one true God. The end result was that God did use him mightily, and because of Paul's faithfulness, many people were brought to the Lord.

In his letter to young Timothy, Paul writes of the foundation of hope for those in need of forgiveness for their past sins. "Christ Jesus came into the world to save sinners – of whom I am the worst. But for that very reason I was shown mercy so that in me, the worst of sinners, Christ Jesus might display His unlimited patience as an example for those who would believe on Him and receive eternal life." (1Timothy 1: 15-16) Are you willing, like Paul, to allow Jesus to work through you and reflect the Son's light to others?

When we speak of forgiveness and second chances, who can forget that bulldog of faith, Peter? Peter was the poster child for hot and cold, of being on fire for the Lord one moment and then turning his back on Him the next. Peter was the brash, impetuous disciple who had big plans for himself. He was a man of faith and he let everyone around him know it. His problem

Hope for Forgiveness

was that he started out as a big talker, but when it came time to hold firm in his beliefs, he was the first one to waver. When Jesus told Peter that he would deny knowing Him, Peter was adamant in denying that possibility. Yet shortly after that he was in fact denying that he ever knew Jesus...not once, but three times. I think of what it must have been like to be in Peter's shoes. We know Jesus by our faith and by what we have studied in the Bible, but Peter actually walked with him, talked with him, ate with him. Jesus was living, breathing flesh and bone before Peter's eyes and Peter had seen the miracles that Jesus had performed. Despite all that, he still denied knowing Him for fear of punishment or death. Can you imagine the shame he must have felt when the reality of what he had done had set in? Who would be able to consider themselves useful as a disciple after that? How can you recover from such a grievous mistake? Peter, however, acknowledged his sin and accepted God's forgiveness. Most importantly, Peter used his past experiences to make him that much more an effective witness for Christ.

I have one question to ask you again. Is there anything in your life that God wouldn't be able and willing to forgive you for? I'm not talking about what *you* are willing to forgive yourself for, although that's an important step in finding the road to hope. Please be reassured. If the depths of God's forgiveness towards you could be measured in terms of brightness, you would be blinded by its light!

The God of Hope

I'll admit that it can be a difficult task accepting God's forgiveness in our life, despite the fact that as Christians we intellectually know this truth. So what do we do when we get it wrong for the umpteenth time? We get up, dust ourselves off, and most importantly repent and accept God's willing forgiveness, compassion and mercy. No one is ever hopeless who is willing to accept God's forgiveness and be embraced by the loving arms of Christ. It's often our own mindset that leads us to the point of hopelessness, not God's condemnation. That may be the biggest stumbling block on our road to hope. Don't be too hard on yourself when searching for hope. God loves you despite your missteps. Even when we fall short, God still loves us. That should give us the greatest comfort of all.

If you still doubt this truth, consider one more example of forgiveness from the New Testament. A crowd has gathered and is accusing a woman of sins associated with prostitution. Jesus is there as well. God's law made it clear that prostitution was definitely sinful behavior. The accusers could then be justified in their condemnation of this woman, and in fact they wanted to stone her to death as punishment. What does Jesus say to the crowd? "He that is without sin among you, let him first cast a stone at her." (John 8:7 KJV) One simple sentence that was exactly what was needed to silence the crowd and send them slinking away. There was no condemnation of this woman by Jesus. She most certainly knew that her lifestyle was not what it should be, yet after the crowd had thinned, what did Jesus say to

Hope for Forgiveness

her? "Go and sin no more." (John 8:11 KJV) That was it, and I'm sure that He said it with the compassion of a father toward a remorseful child. Notice Jesus made it clear to the woman that He knew she was sinning, but His careful admonition to her was wrapped up in a package of mercy and grace.

In the book of Ezekiel, the certainty of God's forgiving nature is made abundantly clear. "But if a wicked man turns away from all the sins he has committed and keeps all My decrees and does what is right and just, he will surely live; he will not die. None of the offenses he has committed will be remembered against him. Because of the righteous things he has done, he will live. Do I take any pleasure in the death of the wicked? declares the Sovereign Lord. Rather, am I not pleased when they turn from their ways and live?" (Ezekiel 18: 21-23)

Consider now for a moment someone who was unwilling or unable to accept the forgiveness of God. Judas was a man who committed probably the most grievous sin of all. He was the individual guilty of betraying Jesus for thirty pieces of silver, and contributing to his Savior's death. I ask you, though…if Judas had come to Jesus and confessed his sin, then begged for Christ's forgiveness, do you honestly believe that Jesus would not have forgiven him? I know in my heart, and I pray that you know in yours, that Jesus would have embraced Judas and forgiven every last one of Judas' sins. The difference between Judas and the aforementioned Biblical heroes is that Judas was unwilling or unable to repent and accept God's forgiveness.

The God of Hope

During the final hours of Jesus' life on earth, He demonstrated His unlimited willingness to forgive even as He was being crucified. Hanging between two true criminals, He said of his accusers and the ones nailing Him to the cross, "Father, forgive them, for they do not know what they are doing." (Luke 23: 34). The two criminals alongside Him provided a strong example of the choice we as sinners have to accept or decline this forgiveness. On the one hand, the unrepentant criminal mocked Jesus. "Aren't you the Christ? Save Yourself and us!" (Luke 23: 39) This man wanted to be saved but he was unwilling to humble himself and repent. The other criminal, however, rebuked the first man. "Don't you fear God, since you are under the same sentence? We are punished justly, for we are getting what our deeds deserve. But this man has done nothing wrong." (Luke 23: 40-41) Then the second man did the one thing needed for his pardon. He humbled himself before Jesus and repented of his life's sin. "Jesus, remember me when You come into Your kingdom." What was Jesus' answer to this repentant man? "I tell you the truth, today you will be with me in paradise." (Luke 23: 42-43)

You see, one of the wonderful things about God is the abundance of grace and mercy that he lavishes on his children. Grace and mercy have often been described in the following terms. Grace is God giving us what we don't deserve, and mercy is God not giving us what we do deserve. Both are free gifts from God and are a daily reminder of how much He loves us despite our failures. So it is with each and every one of us. We are all flawed…burdened by the weight of original sin. Sometimes accepting His forgiveness is the hardest part of it all. Yet we can hold our heads high as we remind ourselves daily that God is always there, waiting with open, loving arms to tell us that it's okay…that He forgives us, and tomorrow is going to be a beautiful day filled with the everlasting hope that only He can give! We are continually being spiritually renewed because of the price Christ paid for our sins on the cross. If God tells you that you can be made new and whole, aren't you going to believe Him? Don't allow yourself to be swayed by the lies of the devil!

It's those very lies of Satan the accuser that can wreak havoc in our walk with God. Satan shouts condemnation, while God often seems to whisper encouragement. There's no question as to who is sovereign in this world and our lives if we would only let Him be. God is there to protect and defend us from the assaults of the devil, when we feel the shame of past sins weighing us down with hopelessness. Some of the most reassuring words regarding the father of lies come from the book of Revelation. There it's revealed the final outcome of the one who seeks to defeat us with the weight of our sin. "And there was war in heaven. Michael and his angels fought against the dragon and the dragon and his angels fought back. But he was not strong enough, and they lost their place in heaven. The great dragon was hurled down- that ancient serpent called the devil of satan, who leads the whole world astray. He was hurled to the earth and his angels with him. Then I heard a loud voice in heaven say, 'Now have come the salvation and the power and the kingdom of our God, and the authority of his Christ. For the accuser of our brethren, who accuses them before our God day and night, has been hurled down. They overcame him by the blood of the Lamb and by the word of their testimony.'" (Revelation 12:7-11) The power of Satan's lies cannot overwhelm the power of God's forgiveness. Never forget that truth!

Remember that song by Matthew West mentioned earlier in this chapter? While the first half of the song describes the struggle with self-condemnation, the second half of the song reveals the real impact of God's forgiveness and mercy on our lives. The song closes with the acknowledgment of Satan's lies, and the confirmation that those lies will no longer be believed. Instead of being known by the names of regret and defeat, the listener is encouraged to become known as the child of God, the one true King. Because of Jesus' death on the cross and His resurrection, we sinners have been absolved of our guilt and forever changed. We have experienced His love and saving grace.

Because of God's forgiveness of our sins, we like St. Paul can be even more motivated to live a life that produces good fruit for God. Because we have experienced the riches of His grace we can face the future with joy and enthusiasm instead of an air of defeat. If you can embrace the wonderful hope that comes with a repentant heart which accepts God's forgiveness, then you can also appreciate what the gift of forgiveness can be to another person in need of it. Have you ever been betrayed or hurt by someone, and deep in your heart you could not let go of the anger or resentment you harbored toward that person? The grudge that you held against the individual was so deeply cemented in your being that it seemed there was no force strong enough to budge it? Well, if you consider how God has forgiven you and then call on His strength to soften your heart, you can find it within yourself to forgive that person, no matter what grievous sin they may have committed against you. On this matter, the Bible is very clear. Ephesians 4:32 states "Be kind and compassionate to one another, forgiving each other, just as in Christ God forgave you." Do you remember the parable that Jesus spoke to His disciples about the unmerciful servant? In Matthew 18, Peter asks Jesus how many times he should forgive his brother when he sins against him. Peter thinks he is being generous when he answers his own question. "Up to seven times?" he quizzes Jesus. Jesus answered Peter, 'not seven times, but seventy-seven times." (Matthew 18:22) Jesus then goes on to describe the actions of the unmerciful servant to illustrate his point. How a servant who owed a great debt to the king had the debt cancelled by his master, but who then ran into an acquaintance who owed him a fraction of what he had owed. What did this man do? Instead of remembering the great debt that had just been forgiven him, he thought only of getting even with the man who owed him, and had that man thrown into prison until he could repay the debt. The end result was that his master found out about his short memory and threw him into prison as well. His lack of forgiveness in the face of receiving such grace led to his personal downfall. Jesus ended His parable with the following warning to His disciples. "This is how my heavenly Father will treat each of you unless you forgive your brother from your heart." (Matthew 18: 35)

Can you recall the story of Joseph and his brothers in the book of Genesis? Joseph, the favored son of his father Jacob, was definitely not favored by his brothers. In fact, Joseph's brothers were so jealous of him that they hatched a plot to be rid of him by selling him into slavery. When you think of how much Joseph suffered because of what his brothers did to him, it wouldn't be hard to imagine that Joseph would be unwilling to forgive the lot of them. Yet Joseph recognized that unwillingness to forgive his siblings was not what God wanted for him. When his brothers threw themselves at his feet and begged for mercy, Joseph responded with these words of wisdom. "You intended to harm me, but God intended it for good to accomplish what is now being done, the saving of many lives (Genesis 50: 20). Joseph acknowledged that it was through his brothers' actions that God had implemented a plan to save his entire family from a devastating famine. Joseph could see the bigger picture and purpose for his past, and knew that forgiveness towards his brothers was his only option. It may not have been the easiest

Hope for Forgiveness

option, but Joseph placed God's command above his own need for vindication. Considering all the sins that God has forgiven us for, are we willing to do the same?

Perhaps one of the greatest examples of the power of forgiveness in relatively recent times involved a woman named Corrie ten Boom. Corrie and her father and sister lived in Holland during World War II. During the war this Dutch family hid and protected many Jews from the Nazis. Eventually the Nazis found out what these three had been doing and they were sent to a concentration camp. It was in this camp that both Corrie's father and sister died. I can imagine Corrie spent every day grieving for her deceased family and wondering if she would be next. She certainly had every right to be fearful for her life and what the Nazi guards would do to her. She survived the camp and the war and went on to give many talks about her ordeal and her relationship to Christ. It was during one of these talks that a familiar face appeared. It was one of the Nazi guards who had been at the same camp as she and her family. He approached her and wanted one thing…her forgiveness! In the time since the war, this former guard had become a Christian and had come to realize the gravity of the evil that he had been a part of. Now knowing Christ, he came to beg Corrie's forgiveness for the part he had had in her family's suffering. Corrie described the inner turmoil she experienced being face to face with this man she had every right to hate. When this man asked Corrie, "Will you forgive me?" Corrie recalled her thoughts. "I could not. I remembered the suffering of my dying sister through him. But when I saw that I could not forgive, suddenly I knew I myself had no forgiveness. Do you know that Jesus had said that? When you do not forgive those who have sinned against you, my heavenly Father will not forgive you your sins. (Matthew 6:15) And I knew oh, I am not ready for Jesus to come real quick because I have no forgiveness for my sins. And I was not able. I could not. I could only hate him." Yet, she knew in her heart that she had no choice but to forgive him as she weighed the forgiveness that Christ had bestowed on her for her failings in life. "And then I took one of these beautiful texts, one of these boundless resources, Romans 5:5…'The love of God is shed abroad into our hearts through the Holy Spirit who is given to us.' And I said, "Thank you Jesus, that you have brought into my heart God's love through the Holy Spirit who is given to me. And thank you Father that Your love is stronger than my hatred and unforgiveness." When she expressed her forgiveness towards this man, she described an unforgettable feeling and presence of God. "That same moment I was free and I could say, Brother, give me your hand and I shook hands with him. And it was as if I felt God's love stream through my arms! You've never touched so, the ocean of God's love, as that you forgive your enemies." My question to you is this…if it had been you in that concentration camp, would you be able to forgive that Nazi guard? Could you? It's only when we fathom the depth of God's forgiveness towards us that we can muster the strength to forgive

Hope for Forgiveness

those who have sinned against us. As God has provided us lasting hope through His forgiveness, we are given the freedom to forgive in like manner. Oh the hope you can give to someone who is longing for that same sense of freedom through your forgiveness! To forgive and be forgiven…that is a reason for hope!

Chapter 6

HOPE FOR THE LONELY AND BROKENHEARTED

"Never will I leave you; never will I forsake you."
Hebrews 13: 5

And surely I am with you always, to the very end of the age.
Matthew 28: 20

    The harsh reality of life is that no one is immune from heartbreak and loss. The circumstances surrounding such grief or loss may differ from person to person, but the pain and emotional suffering that result are often widespread and long lasting. A lonely or broken heart can come in all shapes and sizes. It may come from the loss of someone close to us…perhaps a spouse, child or other family member. It may also come from the loss of a friend or even a pet. While we certainly associate loneliness and grief with the death of a loved one, that isn't the only cause of deep emotional wounds. In some cases, loved ones may not have died but may have abandoned or become estranged from us. Sometimes these shattered relationships can be every bit as painful as that of a loved one's death. Individuals suffering from loneliness may be physically isolated from other people due to old age or illness. Emotional pain from past betrayals may cause people to build up walls that leave them cut off from the rest of the world. Sometimes, a person may even feel profound loneliness despite being in the company of other people. That person may feel that no one understands them or their circumstances in life. Or it may be that life has dealt blow after blow that leaves an individual battered, bruised and ready to give up. Whatever precipitates those feelings of loneliness and grief, the resulting pain can leave one feeling as if their world and their purpose here have been turned upside down. When the grief is overwhelming, it's difficult, if not impossible, to feel that life holds any promise for the future.

Do you know what it feels like to be all alone? Have you personally experienced the despairing crush of loneliness or the painful ache of a broken heart? Chances are that you have. If not, then consider yourself blessed, but chances are also good that you will at some point in the future. You may have seen the loss coming, so that it didn't come as much of a surprise. Or the loss might have come so quickly and unexpectedly that there was no way to prepare for it. I suppose you can make the argument that when you've had time to prepare for a loss like the death of a loved one, the heartbreak may seem a little less severe. Sudden losses, however, not only leave a person immersed in grief but also overwhelmed by shock from the seeming randomness of the event.

Hope for the Lonely and Brokenhearted

It's said that one of the most stressful events in a person's life is the death of a spouse. This certainly makes sense when you consider the lifelong bond that husband and wife commit to on their wedding day. After years of being there for each other, the thought of having to live without their loved one can be crippling to the surviving spouse. This was the person who was to share your life, to be there in good times and bad, to provide support and understanding for you that no one else could provide. The longer the marriage has lasted, the harder it seems to accept a life without the other person. I imagine that for married couples, the hope is that when death comes, it comes for both at the same time, so that one is not left alone. I marvel at God's timing whenever I hear or read about an elderly couple who has been married for five or six decades, and who leave this earth together, through some accident, or simultaneous illness. While that does occasionally happen, more often than not, one member of the lifelong partnership is left to pick up the pieces and face the challenges of the future on their own. That prospect can leave the surviving spouse afraid, embittered and certainly pessimistic about any hope for future happiness.

If the death of a spouse can break one's heart, think for a moment what the death of a child must do to the parents facing that premature loss. I'm sure you've heard it said that no parent should ever outlive their child. For any parent who has faced that pain, the void that is left by their child's absence can be unbearable. It's a parent's job to care for and protect their child.

The God of Hope

When illness or accident takes that young life, inevitably mother or father will feel as if they somehow failed, even though that's most often not the case. Childhood cancer and unpredictable accidents give no warning of the road ahead, but only leave the emptiness of a life cut short.

Such a loss became an unwelcome reality for singer-songwriter Steven Curtis Chapman and his family. In 2008 Steven and his wife Mary Beth lost their young daughter Maria Sue in a tragic accident. Can you imagine the overwhelming grief these parents and the rest of their family experienced, and continue to experience? In a subsequent interview months after the tragedy, Steven and his wife described the feelings they experienced following their profound loss…the initial shock, the anger, the question of why and all the other emotions tied up in the grieving process. Oftentimes the process of emotional survival comes one day at a time, or even minute by minute. Trying to understand why God would bless father and mother with a child, only to take that child away through a tragic accident or illness is one of life's hardest questions to answer.

Steven alluded to the pain of his family's loss in the song entitled "Long Way Home". In this song he speaks of the desire to be home with his heavenly Father and with his daughter, and wishing he could take a "shortcut" home. But as the title suggests, there are often no shortcuts, and God takes us the long way around. The long way around may subject us to painful losses, but eventually we'll reach our eternal destination in heaven. While one may never imagine that life could be so difficult at times, there is still a fervent belief that there is a purpose to the delays and detours that life is so full of. God never allows heartbreak without the reassurance of His guiding hand to accompany us through the grief.

Anyone who has lost a loved one can identify with the sentiment in Steven's song. Have you ever been at a point in your life where the loss consumes you and it seems that storm after storm has come relentlessly against you? Initially you may have tried to ride these storms out, but after a while you begin to wonder if you can ever get out from the cloud you're under. Despite our best efforts, the tragic events in our lives have us spun around, trying to move forward with a broken compass. It may seem as if we're headed in the wrong direction and have lost our way, but God gently reminds us that He is our compass and is leading us the long way home. It may not be the way we planned the road trip of life to go, but the extra miles and apparent detours are part of the refining process in our spiritual maturity. Romans 5:3 reminds us that suffering produces perseverance, perseverance builds character, and character begets hope. To get to that hope, we have to travel the long, rough road. Unfortunately, for most of us there seem to be no shortcuts when it comes to learning the lessons God wants us to learn. Often the way home to the Father has its share of grief, as the Chapman family experienced.

The God of Hope

The sudden loss of a child can produce profound emotional fallout in surviving parents. Consider the raw emotion that accompanied the unexpected loss of the Shunammite woman's son in the Old Testament. This particular woman showed much kindness to the prophet Elisha, feeding him and giving him a place to stay whenever he traveled through her town. Elisha wanted to repay her kindness to him, and asked her what he could do for her. His servant let Elisha know that the woman had no son and that her husband was old. Elisha had discovered the unspoken desire of this woman's heart and asked God to answer her silent prayer. Despite the couple's biological limitations, God intervened and she gave birth to a son the following year. Some time later, when the boy was older he became ill and died. Grieving, this heartbroken mother sought out Elisha. When she found him, she spoke to him with brutal honesty. "Did I ask you for a son, my lord? she asked. Didn't I tell you 'Don't raise my hopes?" (2 Kings 4:28) In other words, "Why would you give me a son if you were only going to take him away from me?" Perhaps her words echo the desperation and anguish you may have felt at your own loss. How can you reconcile the loss of a beloved child with a loving God? And how can hope survive after life has dealt such a crippling blow?

Are you familiar with the nineteenth century hymn, "It is Well with My Soul"? If so, you might first get the impression that the hymn's writer was someone relatively unscathed by life's tragedies. The title of the hymn seems to suggest a sense of

Hope for the Lonely and Brokenhearted

peace in one's life. Yet Horatio Spafford, the hymn's author, wrote its verses after suffering devastating losses. In 1871, he and his family experienced great financial setbacks when their property was destroyed in the great Chicago fire. While certainly a substantial material loss, no one in his family could imagine what lay ahead for them...the loss of four daughters in 1873 and a son in 1880. Originally scheduling a trip overseas with his wife and four daughters in November of 1873, Spafford was unexpectedly delayed in the states over business matters. His wife and daughters, however, continued on the overseas voyage. Several days into the trip, their ship was accidently struck by another vessel and sunk. His wife survived, but all four daughters died. It's said that as he sailed to reunite with his wife overseas, Spafford wrote the words to his hymn as he passed near the spot where his family's ship had reportedly gone down.

In spite of his terrible losses, Spafford chose to focus on the promises of Christ rather than on his pain. The first two verses of his hymn speak to finding that peace that only Christ can bring in the midst of tragedy.

> "When peace, like a river, attendeth my way
> When sorrows like sea billows roll
> Whatever my lot, Thou hast taught me to say
> It is well, it is well, with my soul
>
> Though Satan should buffet, though trials should come

The God of Hope

Lest this blest assurance control
That Christ has regarded my helpless estate
And hath shed His own blood for my soul"

When loneliness and heartbreak result from the loss of a loved one or some other hardship, it's only natural to want to understand why those tragic events have occurred. Human nature wants to know the purpose of the tragedy. We want God to explain to us why and how He could allow such pain into our lives. But one of the most difficult questions that may never be answered in one's lifetime is "Why?". Why was my loved one taken from me? Why did this accident have to happen? What good could ever come from the loss? Human nature demands an answer, but God so often remains silent. Can it be enough for a heartbroken individual to accept that the earthly questions really only have an answer when the focus is on things eternal? The hole that your particular tragedy has created in your heart can only be successfully filled by the great consolation of Jesus Christ. Once that hole is filled, no longer will the pain and loneliness associated with life's losses be able to defeat you. The emptiness that you feel so deeply in your soul can only be replaced by the comfort of a lifelong relationship with God. More than anything God wants that relationship with you, one that extends from the earthly to the eternal. While no one on this earth can answer the question of why bad things have to happen, can you still accept that God is sovereign and that He has a reason for the loneliness and grief that you're suffering? Can you allow that loneliness to point you in the direction of God's loving arms and the comfort of His strength and grace? Can you say with Horatio Spafford, that despite the tragedy, it is well with your soul?

While the death of a loved one can create tremendous suffering for a person, I don't want to minimize the pain that a person can experience because of the hurtful actions of living spouses or other family members and friends. Have you known someone who has had to suffer through the pain of marital infidelity? Perhaps you yourself have been the victim of your spouse's unfaithfulness. Although all too common in this day and age, marital problems and divorce wreak havoc where there once was mutual trust and love. Consider the emotional scars that can result when separation from a spouse is not the result of death but rather abandonment. The sense of rejection that comes from knowing that the person you shared your life with has betrayed the trust you placed in them can have devastating lifelong effects. A heart broken from that disloyalty may never truly heal in this lifetime. Compound that rejection with now having to raise children all on your own and it's not surprising that feelings of isolation and loneliness can develop. It's not easy carrying all of life's burdens without any help. While divorce can have devastating effects on the spouse left behind, consider the emotional scars that it can create in the children of the marriage. Caught in the middle, children are the silent victims who often feel the effects of their parents' battles long into adulthood. Divorce spares no one in the family.

Have you ever been betrayed by a friend or family member? Did their hurtful behavior hit you out the blue and leave you wondering who you could trust? If so, it's perfectly natural to want to guard yourself against further betrayal by walling yourself off from anyone else who might hurt you that way again. In a sense you've created your own well protected island, where no one can come ashore. While that level of self-protection may lower your chances of being hurt again, it also makes for a lonely and painful life. Perhaps you would very much like to remain connected with the rest of the world, but age and physical infirmities have made it difficult, if not impossible, to interact with others the way you once did. Despite your friends' and family's best intentions, the phone calls and visits you rely on don't come as frequently as you think they should. Not only can that create profound loneliness, but it can foster bitterness and resentment as well.

Whatever the cause of your grief or loneliness, the toll it exacts on your spiritual well-being can be devastating. When your spirit is completely worn down, it often seems that there are no coping mechanisms left. Proverbs 18:14 addresses the severity of such a spiritual condition…"The human spirit can endure in sickness, but a crushed spirit who can bear?" It's at this point that one can fall into the trap of thinking that since these crushing blows have been allowed by God, there's no point in turning to Him for relief. Your whys have gone unanswered and your cries for relief have seemingly fallen on God's deaf ears. In the midst of your suffering, though, don't allow your pain to build another wall that separates you from God. You may not see or hear Him, but He is there, even in the midst of this painful life of yours. You can spend the rest of your life searching for answers to explain tragedy and still never find them. The brutal truth is that we live in a fallen world where pain and loss abound. Tragedy does not discriminate. It's no respecter of persons. When it comes, and it will eventually come, how will you deal with it? Will you retreat from the world and try to bury your despair with isolation? Or do you accept your grief and try to move forward in a manner that consciously seeks to align your life within God's will?

Have you heard of the television program, "America's Most Wanted"? For the years that the show was on the air, its' host, John Walsh, worked with viewers and law enforcement agencies to search for and capture more than twelve hundred hardened criminals. Did you know how John came to be involved with the show? His own six year old son, Adam, was abducted and murdered. John certainly had every right to grab hold of his grief and retreat from the world because of his tremendous loss. Instead he chose to take that tragedy and try to bring good from the bad. No one can know how many other parents his efforts spared from a loss like he and his wife suffered. Given the choice between capturing those criminals and having his son back, there's no question that John would choose to have his son with him, alive and well. But having no choice in the matter, John did the best to honor his son's memory and bring purpose to his suffering.

So often we cannot see any purpose in the loss and loneliness. That, however, does not imply that there is no purpose. God, in His omniscience, knows how every tragedy in our lives falls into the pre-ordained plan He has for us. Do you remember the Old Testament story of Ruth and Naomi? Tragedy and loss in their lives led to events that shaped history and eventually led to the birth of Jesus Christ. But those events brought much grief and loneliness to these two women first. Naomi, her husband and two sons were forced to travel from Judah to Moab because of a famine in their homeland. While in Moab, Naomi's husband died and she was left a widow. Her two sons married Moabite women, one of whom was Ruth. After they had lived in Moab about ten years, both of Naomi's sons died. Can you imagine the grief that she must have experienced, having lost her husband and then both her sons? It was small comfort when her daughter-in-law Ruth decided to accompany her back to Judah rather than abandon her to return to her own family. When the two women returned to Judah, people in town wondered if this broken woman could really be Naomi. Naomi's response reflects the depth of her grief and longsuffering…"Don't call me Naomi. Call me Mara, because the Almighty has made my life very bitter. I went away full, but

Hope for the Lonely and Brokenhearted

the Lord has brought me back empty. Why call me Naomi? The Lord has afflicted me; the Almighty has brought misfortune upon me." (Ruth 1:20-21) There was no hiding the bitterness and grief that Naomi continued to feel, and I imagine she must have wondered if there was any purpose for her suffering. It was through the death of her husband and sons, however, that Ruth was led to marry Boaz, one of Naomi's relatives. From that union came a son, Obed, who was the father of Jesse. Jesse, of course, was the father of David, who would later become king of Israel and a direct ancestor of Christ. From Naomi and Ruth's vantage point, their suffering seemed to have no purpose. But from God's vantage point, these tragic events were part of a bigger plan that only He could see. The loss and grief that Naomi and Ruth faced would eventually result in the birth of their Savior!

Like Naomi and Ruth, the person who has lost their spouse has lost love, companionship and physical and emotional intimacy. It was God who gave that married couple to each other. God acknowledged in the Garden of Eden that it was not good for man to be alone, so He created woman. The original couple, Adam and Eve, relied on each other, and that was good. But they were both also meant to rely on God. While marriage is a precious gift from God, it was never meant to take away the true source of comfort and reliance that is available to all of us, whether married or single. My point is certainly not to minimize the heartbreak of losing a spouse. The husband or wife you lost was part of a wonderful bond that was God given and meant to enrich both your lives. But while all earthly bonds will eventually end, the bond that you have with your heavenly Father is everlasting. The comfort that you received from your spouse's love may be gone right now, but the love and solace that God is holding for you existed before your marriage, was intertwined with your marriage, and remains after any loss. Christ remains the bridegroom longing to embrace you and give you the comfort, love and daily assurance that you may feel is no longer available to you since your loss. Are you willing to accept that love and solace that He so freely wants to give? Can you believe that in all things He can restore peace to your lonely and grieving heart?

Through all the tragedies that Job had to endure, he acknowledged that in spite of the pain God was sovereign. Job wisely noted of his circumstances, "The Lord gave, and the Lord hath taken away; blessed be the name of the Lord" (Job 1:21 KJV) Job may never have figured out why the Lord allowed such loss into his life, but he acknowledged that God was ultimately in control of his life's circumstances. Whether or not God brought relief to this righteous man was secondary to Job's need to submit to God's will. If we allow Him to, God can bring solace to the grieving and companionship to the lonely.

Have you witnessed or perhaps personally experienced how God can restore meaning to a life affected by loss or loneliness? I have, and I'm continually amazed by God's resourcefulness and perfect timing. It's comforting to see how God creates new and wonderful friendships that ease the burden of mutual loss. He has a way of perfectly providing friends who, although never being able to replace a loved one, nonetheless bring a new purpose and fulfillment to a grieving person's life. And God not only provides two-legged friends. Sometimes a new friend may have four legs. As an animal lover, I've seen firsthand how pets can help successfully fill the void of loneliness that loss has created in a person's life. The job of caring for a pet brings a sense of purpose where there might have been none, as well as the unconditional love that a pet can provide.

For those of you who are animal lovers, you understand the special bond you have with your pet. I have always imagined myself a dog person. I grew up in a family of dog lovers, and never had a cat. My preconceived notions about cats were that they were too independent and too finicky to be reliable companions. Then a little neighborhood stray changed my admittedly biased opinion about the species. You could say this little fellow adopted me as much as I adopted him. I'm firmly convinced that God led him to me, as he was such a perfect fit for my personality. He came when I called him, would wait at the door for me when I came home from work, and acted more like a dog than I ever imagined a cat could. I have no doubt that God brought him into my life to provide companionship and a measure of joy I had forgotten I needed. That was why it was so hard when suddenly and unexpectedly one morning he got sick, and within twenty-four hours he was gone. The cat who I had grown to love over the course of nine years, who knew my habits and personality perfectly, who anticipated my actions, was no longer there. The stages of grief are every bit as powerful here as with any other loss. The suddenness and speed with which he died left me numb. In the days that followed, I tried to comprehend the whys of what had happened, process the guilt I felt in thinking there should have been something I could have done to prevent his death, and accept his absence in my life. No longer would he whiz past me as I climbed the stairs each night, no soulful begging each time I walked into the kitchen, no more cat naps on my shoulder while I sat on the couch. While there are those who would minimize the loss of a pet compared to the loss of a person, grief is grief, no matter who it's suffered for. While the Bible never discusses the disposition of departed pets, and it's not within the scope of this book to discuss the theological arguments for or against, I like to believe that our loving Father knows the deep and abiding love we have for our animals and that he will make all things right when we arrive in heaven. If the likes of Martin Luther and Billy Graham believe that God would make provision for our pets in heaven, then I believe that God has given our pets as it were, "on loan to us" and when He calls an end to their earthly lives we will one day be reunited with them in heaven.

Hope for the Lonely and Brokenhearted

I guess my point here is to never underestimate the means by which God can bring purpose and fulfillment to a lonely person's life. Psalm 68: 5-6 gives some of the attributes of our heavenly Father. He is "a father to the fatherless, a defender of widows...God sets the lonely in families." And in Psalm 146: 9, "The Lord watches over the alien and sustains the fatherless and the widow." God sees your loneliness and He doesn't want that loneliness to dictate your life. He longs to be the companionship that your soul yearns for.

What source of comfort can the Lord provide after the death of your loved one? The reality is that for the remainder of your earthly existence, the person you loved will be physically absent from your side. How do you reconcile this loss with a kind and compassionate God? Again the answer lies in the eternal, not the earthly. How can we compare what awaits us in heaven with the oh so fleeting life that we know here on earth?

Every so often, I'll read a story about someone who has lost a loved one and is having a difficult time coping with the loss. Then something will happen that provides them reassurance that their loved one is safe in the arms of God. I don't mean to suggest that every single quirky event that grieving individuals encounter after a loss equates to supernatural assurances. But I do believe that God is very much in tune with our grief and that He at times will orchestrate an event or events to provide some measure of earthly comfort to those individuals who have been affected by the loss.

The God of Hope

If we're searching for the reassurance of eternal glory, I can think of no better example than the Biblical story of Lazarus. This story should help give us a glimpse of the hope that even earthly death cannot take from us. Lazarus, the beloved friend of Jesus and cherished brother of Mary and Martha, is dead. His two sisters are overwhelmed with grief and overcome by raw emotion. It seems that not even Jesus could intercede on this friend's behalf. Jesus, the son of God who could have spared this family the pain of death, does nothing for four days. By the time he arrives and meets with Mary and Martha, Lazarus' death must have been reluctantly accepted by his sisters. After four days and the natural decomposition process of the human body, Lazarus was beyond being revived...or so it would seem. Mary and Martha could not hide their disappointment, and perhaps even a bit of resentment, toward Jesus. "Lord, if you had been here, my brother would not have died." (John 11: 21) This might be loosely translated to, "Lord, why didn't you do something to prevent this?" Despite their grief, these sisters knew that God could give Jesus whatever He asked for. Even they didn't think that meant an earthly resurrection, though. When Jesus said to Martha, "Your brother will rise again" (John 11: 23), she responded with the acknowledgement that Lazarus would rise again in the resurrection of the last day. It's what Jesus said to her next that should give us all the hope we need to see us through whatever losses we may face in our lives. "I am the resurrection and the life. He who believes in Me will live, even though he dies; and whoever lives and believes in Me will never die." (John 11: 25-26) This one statement is the foundation of our Christian faith and the reason we have hope in the face of loss! Jesus is the embodiment of everlasting life and our living hope. Once Mary and Martha understood this, they had all they needed to face whatever life threw at them. Believing this, Jesus could now provide their brother with the earthly resurrection they had originally hoped for.

Nowadays, we certainly don't expect Lazarus-like resurrections to occur as they did while Jesus walked the earth. However, modern day "miracles" are still happening which underscore the hope of our future eternal resurrection. In February of 2014, Walter Williams, aged seventy-eight years, was pronounced dead by the local coroner after being found by his family with no pulse. Having been confronted with this devastating reality, his family began making funeral arrangements. The following morning, however, funeral workers found Mr. Williams kicking his legs in the body bag. This man, who had been declared dead the night before, was in fact very much alive! Call it a modern day miracle or medical mix-up, a man who had been thought dead was now alive. Can you imagine the incredible, unspeakable joy that members of his family must have experienced upon hearing the news that their loved one was still with them? When interviewed, members of his family called his "second chance at life a gift from God." His daughter had this to say, "I don't know how much longer He's

The God of Hope

(God) going to grace us and bless us with his (her father's) presence, but Hallelujah, we thank Him right now." Walter's daughter had it right. Grateful for the gift of an earthly second chance, she acknowledged the finite aspect of human life and was thankful for the days that the Lord had given her beloved father. Her comfort came in knowing that had her father truly died on that day, he would enter life eternal because of his belief in his Savior. One can only imagine that their feelings must have paralleled the joy that Mary and Martha felt when Jesus raised their brother Lazarus from the grave! Few of us on this earth could probably say that they have experienced such an incredible earthly reunion with loved ones that have died. It's something we would all wish for when the pain of loss becomes too much for us to bear. The reality is that we may never experience what this family experienced with their relative. As real as the pain of loss is, we must focus on the incomprehensible joy that will be ours when we are finally reunited with our loved ones in heaven. As lonely and brokenhearted as we may be right now, living in the void of a missing loved one, the prospect of that blessed reunion for those who have died in Christ holds the greatest blessing and the most profound hope that we could dare to imagine. Just think about it… that heavenly reunion will never end! There will be no more separation from the ones we love, no more good-byes, no more loneliness and heartache. Now that's a reason to be filled with hope!

Hope for the Lonely and Brokenhearted

It's the world's cruel reality that loved ones die before we want them to. I remember watching a scene near the end of the movie, "Forrest Gump". Forrest is standing at the grave of his lifelong love Jenny and expresses his grief with typical honest simplicity. He acknowledges what he learned from his mother, that death is a part of life, but immediately counters with a wish that that weren't the case. Can't we say the same thing? Wouldn't it be wonderful if none of us had to face the loss of someone we loved? But ever since the fall of man in the Garden of Eden, death has become our unwelcome companion. No one escapes it. It doesn't seem to matter how or what the specifics of a loved one's death are. If death is sudden and unexpected, we grieve because we didn't have more time with those we loved. If death was a long, drawn out process we grieve because they had to suffer so. If young, we feel they were cheated of life. If old, we try to comfort ourselves and each other by saying that at least the deceased had lived a good long life. But the bottom line is that they are gone from our lives. So the greatest consolation is to know that the ones we loved died believing in their Savior. The most precious gift you can give someone you love is the message of the Gospel. What an assurance that message provides, knowing that any separation from loved ones is temporary. The sweetest consolation is the reassurance of that blessed reunion with loved ones in heaven. Are you willing to make the effort to ensure that you will one day have that long awaited reunion with those most precious to you?

The God of Hope

My grandfather was one of the most honorable, kind and decent men that I have ever known. He was raised in the Catholic church, but somewhere along the way and for whatever reason he had grown cynical of the church and its practices. I remember as a child that he would come to church with the rest of the family on Christmas, Easter and special occasions. Looking back, though, I think he went more to keep peace within my family than for a genuine desire to worship the Lord. I remember being a teenager at the time, and somehow getting into a conversation with him about religion. That didn't happen very often. In fact, it was the only conversation about religion I can ever remember having with him. He told me that by the time I turned fifteen years old I would abandon the church. I couldn't figure out why he had this hostility toward the church, but I was still at a tender enough age that I was more concerned about disrespecting or angering my grandfather than arguing with him over the eternal disposition of his soul. I was young enough to not fully comprehend what faith and grace meant. Certainly, if good works could earn you a place in heaven, my grandfather would have been at the front of the line through the heavenly gates. But Ephesians 2: 8-9 clearly shows us that this is not the case. Good works don't pave the way to heaven. Instead, salvation is a free gift from God that comes as a result of God's grace through faith in his son Jesus Christ. It doesn't matter how good you may have been in this life: salvation is not a works-based proposition. Your loved ones need to know that

Hope for the Lonely and Brokenhearted

fundamental truth. I've grieved over the possibility that my grandfather's feelings toward the earthly church may have prevented him from accepting God's grace and entering the kingdom of heaven. I regret not being bold enough to have talked with him about the Lord. But I take some comfort in knowing that during his final days he relived some of his early years in the church and remembered long lost spiritual lessons. I hope that in those last hours he re-embraced that faith that he once had, and my real hope is that he will be one of the first ones to greet me when I leave this earthly life.

To those who are heavily burdened with the weight of loneliness and the grief of loss right now, please know that God has not forgotten you! As painful as your situation may be, you are not alone, and you never will be as long as you have your heavenly Father. Your hope can rest in the assurance that His love has not escaped the survivor or the neglected on this earth. The universal need to love and be loved can be satisfied best by your relationship with Jesus Christ. You, as an individual, are worth more to God than all the gold or precious jewels in this world. In John 15:13, we learn what true love is. "Greater love has no one than this, that He lay down his life for His friends." You are that friend that the Bible talks about. Jesus loved you enough that He sacrificed his life for you! That alone should provide tremendous comfort in your loneliness and pain. More than anything, this reassurance of divine love can provide the inspiration and strength to face another day. While human love may have brought us disappointment and heartache, the love of our heavenly Father is a love that is everlasting. It's unearned, a free gift that is with us every single day of our lives if only we are willing to accept it. Can you imagine that there was someone who died over two thousand years ago with you in mind? That is some kind of love!

If you're willing to accept and experience the purest form of love that God has for you, can you live your life with the eternal in mind for those family and friends that are still here with you? For those who know or have already died in Christ, the work is done. But for those who do not yet know or accept the Lord, there is still much work to do. Are you willing to ensure that your loved ones can one day claim their place in heaven because they've come to know and believe in Christ as the one true resurrection and life? The best gift you can give your loved ones is the message and hope of the Gospel! Working toward that spiritual goal can help bring deeper meaning to your current circumstances. For both you and the new believer in Jesus Christ, it is that saving knowledge which affords the truest hope and the greatest peace in this life.

Chapter 7

FAITH – HOPE'S COUSIN

"Now faith is being sure of what we hope for and certain of what we do not see"
Hebrews 11:1

"The righteous will live by faith"
Romans 1: 17

In our search for hope in this life, we often assume that the most important piece of the puzzle is what we can provide through our own efforts. The essence of true hope, though, is in what God can provide through His power, not ours. Our God of hope is the authentic source of the joy and peace that we long to experience in our lives, and it's by the power of the Holy Spirit that we are to be filled with lasting hope. Still, we do have some responsibility in the journey. Our mindset must be such that we believe and eagerly anticipate receiving what God has promised us. In short, we need faith.

What exactly is faith and how does it relate to hope? If you're looking for a good answer to this question, one of the best places to explore in the Bible is the eleventh chapter of Hebrews. You might call this chapter the "Faith Hall of Fame." In it we read about all those individuals who followed God's direction for their lives, even when the road ahead seemed so dark and uncertain. The first verse in the chapter describes faith as "being sure of what we hope for and certain of what we do not see". That's a concise sentence but it packs quite a punch. Faith is being <u>sure</u> of what we hope for? On any given day, can you say that you are absolutely sure about most things? Faith is not being reasonably sure or almost sure of what we hope for, but being <u>absolutely</u> certain of what we hope for. I have a small plaque hanging on a wall in my home that states it quite nicely…"Faith is not believing that God *can*, but knowing that He *will*". Do you have such an absolute faith, or does your faith need a little fine tuning?

By extension, faith is being certain of what we do not see. It's a lot easier to believe in someone or something that we can see, feel and touch. It gets harder to have faith when we're expected to believe what we've never seen with our own eyes. Most of us can say we have never seen God. It requires faith to believe that He exists, and perhaps even more faith to believe that He actually cares for us as individuals. You might ask why an all-knowing and all-powerful God would be concerned with someone like you or me. Here I love St. Augustine's take on the subject…"God loves each of us as if there were only one of us".

If you read through the eleventh chapter of Hebrews, you'll find familiar persons of great faith, but also those individuals who weren't as well known. None of those

Faith – Hope's Cousin

mentioned in this chapter were perfect people. They made their mistakes along the way, but they were commended because they saw through the eyes of faith, and relied on one greater than themselves. There was no long range weather forecast for Noah to rely on, yet at God's command he devoted tremendous time and energy to build an ark that would protect his family from a flood, the likes of which mankind had never before seen. By faith Moses and the Israelites left Egypt for the promise of their own land, despite the strength of the Egyptian army which was standing in their way. Through God's direct intervention they were able to cross the Red Sea unharmed, while the entire Egyptian army was drowned when it tried to cross that same body of water. By faith Abraham moved to a foreign land, became a father when everyone thought it was impossible, and was even willing to later sacrifice his precious son Isaac at God's request. Abraham's faith was "credited to him as righteousness" (Genesis 15:6) because at times it stood out so boldly. In the book of Romans, the apostle Paul elaborates on this faith of Abraham and what God was able to accomplish because of it. "Against all hope, Abraham in hope believed and so became the father of many nations." (Romans 4:18). Doesn't that say it all about the importance of faith? Against all hope, Abraham *in hope* believed! What does "against all hope" mean, after all? Isn't it that all our human reasoning says that there are no possibilities, no outs, no good answers for whatever challenges we might be facing? Faith chooses to embrace the possibilities of

God. Faith is the active decision to choose to believe what God says rather than what the world has to say about the situation. Paul goes on to further describe Abraham's physical but not spiritual limitations. "Without weakening in his faith, he faced the fact that his body was as good as dead – since he was about a hundred years old – and that Sarah's womb was also dead. Yet he did not waver through unbelief regarding the promise of God, but was strengthened in his faith and gave glory to God, being fully persuaded that God had power to do what He had promised." (Romans 4:19-20) For any parent reading this, just think about the energy it requires to have and raise a child, even in the prime of life. Can you imagine having a child when you're as old as Abraham or Sarah was? I'm exhausted just thinking about it! He may have hit a few detours along the way, but for the most part Abraham trusted that God could do what He said He could. Because of that Abraham will forever be known as the "father of many nations".

Of all the requirements for a truly successful Christian life, faith is probably one of the most important. Hebrews 11:6 elaborates on the necessity of faith in one's spiritual life. "Without faith it is impossible to please God, because anyone who comes to Him must believe that He exists and that He rewards those who earnestly seek Him". Throughout the New Testament there are many instances where the faith of the individual was commended. One such incident should give us all

Faith – Hope's Cousin

comfort, especially when we feel our level of faith isn't quite where it should be.

Jesus was out amongst the people and a crowd had gathered around Him. In that crowd was a man whose son was possessed by an unclean spirit. The boy's father told Jesus that he had brought the child to the disciples to be healed, but that the disciples were not able to heal the boy. Jesus asked the father a few questions, which the man answered. This father then said to Jesus, "If You can do anything, take pity on us and help us." Jesus replied, "If you can? …Everything is possible for him who believes." Immediately the boy's father exclaimed, "I do believe; help me overcome my unbelief!" (Mark 9:23-24) What an incredibly honest statement from this desperate father! He knew of Jesus' reputation…that's why he brought his son to Him for healing. He had enough faith to seek out Jesus. But he was honest enough to admit that his faith wasn't where it needed to be. He knew he couldn't tackle this problem on his own, so he did the wisest thing he could possibly do. He called out to Jesus for help! Oh, that we could follow this man's example in our own lives. Our faith may not be worthy of a place in history, but faith in the one true God will bring us closer to that hope for which we are searching.

Bartimaeus was another man in the New Testament whose faith was to be admired. When Jesus and his disciples were on their way out of Jericho, Bartimaeus, who was blind, was sitting by the side of the road begging. When he heard that

Jesus was nearby, he began shouting "Jesus, son of David, have mercy on me!" Those nearby told him to be quiet, but the book of Mark states that this bold blind man shouted all the more, "Son of David, have mercy on me!" Jesus called to Bartimaeus and he came. The question Jesus asked Bartimaeus was this: "What do you want me to do for you?" Bartimaeus replied, "Rabbi, I want to see." What was Jesus' answer? "Go... your faith has healed you." Immediately Bartimaeus received his sight and followed Jesus along the road. (Mark 10: 46-52)

Like Bartimaeus, the Canaanite woman with the demon possessed daughter demonstrated a faith that prompted Jesus to act on her behalf. This woman was not even Jewish, so she was considered somewhat of an outcast. Yet she knew there was something holy about Jesus. She cried out to Him, "Lord, Son of David, have mercy on me! My daughter is suffering terribly from demon possession." This is where Jesus appears to play hard ball with her, but she refuses to be discouraged. Jesus did not respond to her plea at first. In fact, His disciples urged Him to send her away because they thought she was making a nuisance of herself. Jesus finally answered her, "I was sent only to the lost sheep of Israel." So she came to Him and knelt at His feet. "Lord, help me!" she cried out. Jesus responded, "It is not right to take the children's bread and toss it to their dogs." Had Jesus answered your cry for help like that, would you have been rebuffed or would your faith have motivated you to persevere? This woman pressed on. "Yes, Lord...but even the dogs eat the

Faith – Hope's Cousin

crumbs that fall from their master's table." Jesus replied to this persistent mother, "Woman, you have great faith! Your request is granted." And her daughter was healed from that very hour. (Matthew 15: 21-28)

One might read this story about the Canaanite woman and think that Jesus was being incredibly harsh to her. After all, this mother was only pleading on behalf of her daughter. Had she turned away and not been as persistent as she had, would her daughter have been healed? We don't know the answer to that. But the message is clear. We need to have the persistence and faith in our daily lives that this woman had. It's an attitude that embraces a relentless focus on Christ and doesn't know the meaning of the word quit. Like the woman in Luke 18, who tirelessly approached the merciless judge for justice, we need to remain steadfast in our prayers and firmly convinced that a life of faith in Christ will produce a harvest of spiritual maturity.

Do you remember the woman with the bleeding problem you read about in chapter four? She had a faith in Jesus that made all the difference in her life. Having suffered horribly for twelve years, she sought out Jesus because she thought, "If I just touch his clothes, I will be healed (Mark 5: 28). How is that for faith? What she had hoped for as a result of her faith in the Savior came true. She was instantly healed. Jesus' words to this woman emphasize the power of that faith in Him…"Daughter, your faith has healed you. Go in peace and be freed from your suffering." (Mark 5: 34) Aren't those words we all long to hear?

The God of Hope

How about the friends of the paralyzed man described in the second chapter of Mark? Jesus' reputation at this point in His ministry was so great that a large crowd had surrounded Him, making it virtually impossible for the paralyzed individual to get close enough to Jesus to be healed. We don't know the degree of faith that this afflicted fellow had, but the faith of his friends was noteworthy. These four friends were not in the least deterred by the crowd and the challenge it represented. One way or another, they were going to get Jesus to heal their friend! How did they do it? They climbed up on the roof of the building where Jesus was preaching, and they dug through it so that they could lower the mat their friend was lying on into the sight of Jesus. I wonder what that crowd of people must have thought when they saw a hole open up in the roof and this man being lowered down right in front of Jesus. That's what I call "bulldog" faith! The Bible says that "when Jesus saw their faith, he said to the paralyzed man, 'Son, your sins are forgiven.'" (Mark 2:5) From that moment their friend was healed. Now that's the kind of friends to have!

Another striking example of "all-out" faith in the New Testament is that of the Roman centurion and his sick servant. Here was this centurion who wasn't even an Israelite, yet knew of Jesus' reputation. He sent some Jewish elders to Jesus to request that his servant be healed. As Jesus headed to meet with this man, the centurion sent friends to intercept Jesus with the following message. "Lord, don't trouble yourself, for I do not

Faith – Hope's Cousin

deserve to have You come under my roof. That is why I did not even consider myself worthy to come to You. But say the word and my servant will be healed. For I myself am a man under authority, with soldiers under me. I tell this one, 'Go, and he goes'; and that one, 'Come, and he comes'. I say to my servant, 'Do this', and he does it." (Luke 7:6-8) An important consideration here is that this man knew how he compared to Jesus. As a Roman centurion, he had every cultural right to feel superior to this Jewish carpenter. Yet he humbled himself and acknowledged with respect the authority of the living God. His faith declared that Jesus was so powerful He didn't even have to be near the sick servant to heal him. All this faith from a Gentile! Jesus commended this sincere and faithful centurion. Luke described the Lord's reaction. "When Jesus heard this, He was amazed at him, and turning to the crowd following Him, He said, 'I tell you, I have not found such great faith even in Israel.'" (Luke 7:9) Wouldn't you love for Jesus to be able to say that about you?

If you were to look honestly at yourself, and evaluate how much faith you have, what would the numbers look like? Would your faith be in the top percentile, or at the bottom of the ranking? It's okay to admit that your faith isn't where it needs to be or where you would like it to be. It's a starting point, and with God's help and guidance, you can grow that faith. Like blind Bartimaeus and the Canaanite woman, our prayer can be "Son of David, have mercy on us."

The God of Hope

Have you ever thought that if you just had enough faith, anything would be possible? After all, isn't that what it says in the Bible..."If you have faith as small as a mustard seed, you can say to this mountain, 'Move from here to there' and it will move. Nothing will be impossible for you." (Matthew 17:20-21) Joshua had that type of faith as he led the Israelites into the promised land. What God commanded, he carried out, even if it didn't seem to make great sense. Arriving at the city of Jericho, God informed Joshua that He would give the city into the Israelite's hands. But He had a special set of instructions for Joshua to follow before that would happen. He told Joshua, "March around the city once with all the armed men. Do this for six days. Have seven priests carry trumpets of rams' horns in front of the ark. On the seventh day, march around the city seven times, with the priests blowing the trumpets. When you hear them sound a long blast on the trumpets, have all the people give a loud shout; then the wall of the city will collapse and the people will go up, every man straight in." (Joshua 6:3-5) Does this sound like any legitimate battle plan to you? How would walking around a city and blowing trumpets accomplish a military victory? Joshua didn't hesitate for a moment. He faithfully obeyed the Lord's command, and the walls of Jericho did collapse. Faithful obedience to God assured Joshua the victory.

While it would seem at times that faith can make all the difference in determining the outcome of our prayers, we nonetheless need to be careful of taking faith and making it the

Faith – Hope's Cousin

sole determinant of a situation's final outcome. Despite our level of faith, any situation in our life is ultimately determined by the sovereignty of God. He is the ultimate decision maker in whether our prayers are answered in the manner we hope for. Great heartbreak and confusion can occur when we place our level of faith above the will of God. How many people have approached God with the fullest measure of faith, and then turned away from Him when they felt their prayers weren't answered? They may have said, "I had faith, I prayed relentlessly to God for healing…so why didn't God heal my loved one?" Or "If only I had had more faith, God would have changed the outcome of this bad situation". If things don't go right in your eyes it may not be because of your lack of faith. In the end it is God's will that prevails. Prayer may change things, but God makes the ultimate decision. We cannot bend God's will to our own, but must accept what His will dictates for our lives.

    Consider the situations of Naaman and St. Paul, two men from the Old and New Testaments, respectively. Naaman was the army commander of the king of Aram, and he had leprosy, an incurable skin disease. He had heard about the prophet Elisha and was told that Elisha could heal him of his leprosy. Naaman had enough faith to seek out Elisha. But when Elisha sent him a message instructing him to wash seven times in the Jordan River so that he would be healed, his faith hit a brick wall. Naaman angrily responded, "Are not Abana and Pharpar, the rivers of Damascus, better than any of the rivers of Israel? Couldn't I wash in them and be cleansed?" (1 Kings 5:12) Had it not been for Naaman's servants convincing him to follow Elisha's instructions, he wouldn't have been cured. Reluctantly, however, he did wash himself in the Jordan seven times, and he was healed of the leprosy. Clearly, it was not his great faith that made the difference in the outcome here. St. Paul, on the other hand, was someone of great faith. After dedicating his life to serving Jesus, he followed the Lord's leading with great devotion. But as we learned earlier, Paul was nonetheless afflicted by a "thorn in the flesh". This loyal servant of God prayed fervently for God to relieve him of this burden, but God's answer was no. God made it clear to Paul that in this instance, faith was not the determining factor in the outcome. Despite his great faith, it was not God's will for Paul to be healed. To his credit, Paul accepted God's will for what it was, and in fact saw a greater purpose for his suffering…reliance on the strength of his Savior when his own strength was insufficient for the day's challenges. Are we able to look at our suffering and hardship through the eyes of faith like Paul did?

If you or someone you know is a fan of NFL football, you've no doubt heard of Tim Tebow. This former quarterback passionately displayed his Christian faith through words and actions on and off the football field. In doing so, he became somewhat of a lightning rod for differing opinions regarding Christians' expression of faith in the secular world. If you followed his football career, you know that he went through

Faith – Hope's Cousin

some rough times in the league. Despite his struggles, Tim remained strong in his belief that the Lord was guiding his steps, and made it clear that his priority in life was following God's lead. One of his favorite sayings is an oft quoted phrase among Christians…"I don't know what my future holds, but I know who holds my future. His faith was tested when he was cut by the NY Jets, and was without a team. Tim held onto his faith despite an uncertain future and relentless mocking by his critics. How did he respond to these setbacks? By tweeting the wisdom of Proverbs 3:4-6, "Trust in the Lord with all your heart and lean not on your own understanding; in all your ways acknowledge him and he shall direct your paths." He held on to his faith when most around him were saying that he should give up. Then the New England Patriots invited him to their training camp. Things seemed like they were looking up for Tim. Was his faith finally paying off on this rollercoaster ride? It seemed so. Tim didn't make the final roster. Once again it seemed like his last chance had come and gone. Other individuals might have thrown in the towel at this point. The odds were stacked against him. Instead of giving up, Tim spent the next eighteen months relearning his mechanics and putting in the groundwork to make himself a better quarterback. Some might call that foolhardy, but I contend that his actions demonstrated a tremendous level of faith. After all that apparently wasted effort, the Philadelphia Eagles called for him. Finally, it seemed as if Tim's chance to play the sport he loved had come. Even that opportunity fell through, as he was

The God of Hope

cut by the team. For someone who had worked so tirelessly to achieve his goals, it must have been difficult to accept that all his efforts didn't produce the desired result. But this man of faith made it clear that in the grand scheme of things, football was a low priority when compared with the things of God. All the while, Tim continued to reflect the light of Christ through his charitable work with the developmentally challenged, the sick and the disadvantaged. Those he has helped have undeniably been more blessed by his acts of Christian love than anything he could have accomplished on a football field. When it became clear to him that a career in football was not to be, Tim set his sights on becoming a professional baseball player! Opening himself up again to ridicule from critics and skeptics, his attitude has been one of chasing God given dreams and taking each day with faith in the Lord's direction. Against the odds, he was signed by the New York Mets (who themselves faced much criticism for the signing) and is working to realize his new dream. Whether or not a Major League baseball career becomes a reality for Tim, he continually exemplifies his priority of working for the Lord. In doing so, he has been a role model to many individuals and vividly demonstrates the power of faith to a very cynical world. His life thus far has been a wonderful example of the amazing things that can happen with an unwavering faith in the one true Hope!

How exactly does faith factor into how we respond to the hardships of life? How does it help us hold onto the hope that

Faith – Hope's Cousin

God promises? Part of the answer can be found in the book of James. James writes, "Consider it pure joy, my brothers, whenever you face trials of many kinds, because you know that the testing of your faith develops perseverance. Perseverance must finish its work so that you may be mature and complete, not lacking anything. If any of you lacks wisdom, he should ask God, who gives generously to all without finding fault and it will be given to him. (James 1: 2-6) I admit that sometimes it seems like a stretch to look joyfully at the hardships in life. When life has beaten you down, it's a lot easier to be angry at God for letting these bad things happen to us. What we all need to remember is that there is a purpose behind the suffering, and it's for the good of our spiritual maturity that God allows these things to happen to us. Someone once said, "Faith makes things possible, not easy." Doesn't that ring so true? Faith helps us maintain a perspective that focuses on the eternal, not the here and now. "Blessed is the man who perseveres under trial, because when he has stood the test, he will receive the crown of life that God has promised to those who love Him." (James 1:12). How do we persevere under trial? As the author of Hebrews writes, "Let us fix our eyes on Jesus, the author and perfecter of our faith, who for the joy set before Him endured the cross, scorning its shame, and sat down at the right hand of the throne of God. Consider Him who endured such opposition from sinful men, so that you will not grow weary and lose heart." (Hebrews 12:2-3). Here I like to take a cue from someone small

The God of Hope

but steadfast…the ant. If you look at an ant, it's one of the smallest insects in our everyday world. Yet that small insect is one that is praised in the Bible for its unwavering work ethic and perseverance. Proverbs 30:24-25 describes the ant this way…"Four things on earth are small, yet they are extremely wise: ants are creatures of little strength, yet they store up their food in the summer. If you have ever been faced with an invasion of ants in your kitchen during the summer months, you have to be amazed by their tenacity. They have a singular focus, that of searching for and providing food for their colony. They are undeterred by most attempts to get rid of them. Oh, they may scatter when you try to shoo them away, but it isn't long before they're right back on the counter, searching for any crumbs you may have neglected to clean off. Of course they're not guided by any level of faith, as it's an inborn drive that keeps them focused on their task. But if the tiniest ant without faith can accomplish so much, can't we with a little bit of faith do the same? Even if we fall short, we can take comfort, for "if we are faithless, he will remain faithful". (2 Timothy 2:13)

If hope is being able to look at the future through eyes that see a better tomorrow, then faith is the vehicle that helps us stay on the right road. In order to grasp the certainty of hope that is directly linked to belief in our Savior, we must believe that He exists, that He loves us enough to have died and risen for us, and that He wants us to see the future with eyes on the eternal horizon. Faith allows us that vision.

Faith – Hope's Cousin

Imagine this scenario. You're alone in the desert and have been there for days. You're surrounded by hot sand, searing sun, and a canteen that has very little water left in it. You continue on as best you can, searching for any oasis, but day after day you just face more sand and sweltering heat. The only shelter you find is a solitary outcropping of rocks. It's not much but at least it provides a tiny amount of shade from the blistering sun. You realize that you can't survive in this desert much longer. You strain your eyes looking for any sign of life on the far horizon. Suddenly you see what looks like a line of palm trees in the distant landscape. In your state of fatigue, you can't be sure if they're real or only a mirage. Now you're faced with a decision. Do you stay where you are, with some limited protection, and hope for a rescue? Maybe if you get lucky, a friendly camel will wander by with water and a roadmap out of that desert. If those trees are in fact a mirage, the trip to get to them will likely finish you off. But if they're real, there is surely water there, and maybe other travelers to boot. What do you decide to do? Faith is stepping away from the rocks and heading for those trees, believing that no matter what's waiting for you, God is right there with you. Being a movie buff, I love the scene in "Indiana Jones and the Last Crusade", where Indiana has a critical choice to make. His father has just been mortally wounded. Indy's only chance of saving him is to find the chalice of the Holy Grail, with its lifesaving water. The only problem is that the cave that contains the chalice lies on the opposite side of

The God of Hope

a treacherous ravine, and there's no bridge to get across...or at least not one that can be seen by the human eye. All Indiana can see is what looks like a steep ledge that drops off into a bottomless chasm. He's smart enough to realize that the distance between where he is and where he needs to be is too great for him to jump. His face reveals utter desperation as he gazes across the chasm, knowing that if he can't get across his father will die. Then it hits him...he knows what he must do. He utters the answer to the final step in this quest for the Holy Grail. "It's a leap of faith!" While Indy doesn't know for sure whether this invisible bridge will hold his weight, he nonetheless steps out in faith. When he does, he finds that the bridge does support him. Then he is able to cross the ravine, find the chalice and save his father. It's kind of like the Israelite priests at the Jordan River, when they were ready to cross into the Promised Land. There they were, at the river's edge, looking longingly at the opposite shore. But God didn't stop the flow of the river so they could cross it. Facing its dangerous fury, they first had to take the step of faith into the raging current before God stopped the river's flow.

When you're in the midst of despair, it can be difficult, if not impossible, to take that first step of faith. Yet in order to grasp the hope that God longs to give, faith is a vital prerequisite. Real hope lies at the foot of Christ's cross, and faith is the vehicle that helps propel us toward the cross. It's not a faith in our own strength or abilities. It's a faith in our ever dependable,

Faith – Hope's Cousin

always present God. You can't physically see Him, yet faith dictates that you believe in Him. God doesn't expect us to be perfect in our walk of faith, but He is most pleased when we make it our life's work to seek Him. The reward that God promises to those who seek Him may not be what a person expects. The reward that is above all others is the promise of eternal salvation through belief in the Father, Son, and Holy Spirit.

Chapter 8

DOUBT – HOPE'S SABOTEUR

But when you ask Him, be sure that you really expect Him to answer, for a doubtful mind is as unsettled as a wave of the sea that is driven and tossed by the wind.
James 1: 6 NLT

I am the Lord, the God of all mankind. Is anything too hard for Me?
Jeremiah 32: 27

Have you ever noticed the very human tendency of wanting to do everything in life on our own? We strive to be self sufficient, not having to rely on anyone else for anything. From childhood to adulthood, the lessons we learn seem to pull us in a direction opposite of where we really need to be. While God's compass points north, we do everything in our power to head south. Instead of taking God's promises as proof of His willingness to care for us, we instead question His assurance of the same. In a word, we doubt.

If faith can be considered hope's "cousin", then doubt might well be considered the "black sheep of the family." Mountains may be moved by faith, but bottomless pits are dug by doubt. Doubt is that little unrelenting, all pervasive whisper that tells you that God can't be trusted. It's the constant refrain that God isn't going to make things better, and that if you want your life to improve, you're going to have to make it happen on your own. While God is telling you to be still before Him, doubt is telling you to hurry up and forget about God…the only way out is to find your own solution.

Sometimes doubt can seem downright rational. Difficult situations require creative answers. You can often convince yourself that God is nudging you to take one path or another, when in fact it may not be God nudging you at all. Have you ever had to decide between two jobs, or whether to stay or move from where you're currently living? Can you listen closely enough to what the still small voice of God may be trying to tell you, or do you forge ahead after the flip of a coin? You may think you're in the spot God wants you to be in, but the difficulties and challenges you're facing seem so insurmountable that they have you questioning everything. From where you're standing the future looks pretty bleak. There isn't much hope to hold on to, and the prospect of finding any in your current situation looks grim. So do you hold firm and trust that God is working something greater in your life, or do you step away and head off in a different direction? Ultimately, a decision has to be made, but remember that the best decisions are made without doubting God's love or His ability to make things right in your life. Otherwise, we step further away from the hope that God

Doubt – Hope's Saboteur

intends for us. When doubt causes us to forfeit God's hope in favor of our own, oftentimes our situation gets worse, not better.

Moses was a man handpicked by God to lead the Israelite nation out of Egypt. When you read about his life in the Old Testament, would you consider him to be more a man of faith or doubt? To his credit, he did make it through some pretty tough challenges and remained dedicated to God's calling. But even this humble man of God had his doubts. I suppose having to deal with the continually grumbling crowd he oversaw on a daily basis would weaken anyone's resolve. Still, seeing God's presence in the form of a pillar of cloud or fire, and having manna supplied every day should keep one's faith bolstered, shouldn't it? After more complaining from the restless Israelites, Moses' defenses start to break down. Tired of manna, the people are demanding other food. Moses has had it, and like we often do, cries out to God after trying to shoulder the weight of his problems by himself. "Why have You brought this trouble on Your servant? What have I done to displease You that You put the burden of all these people on me? Did I conceive all these people? Did I give them birth? Why do You tell me to carry them in my arms, as a nurse carries an infant, to the land You promised on oath to their forefathers? Where can I get meat for all these people? They keep wailing to me, 'Give us meat to eat!' I cannot carry all these people by myself; the burden is too heavy for me. If this is how You are going to treat me, put me to death right now – if I have found favor in Your eyes – and do not let me face my own ruin." (Numbers 11:11-15) Moses is really unloading a lot of pent-up frustration. It seemed as if he had reached his breaking point, and the floodgates of his anger, doubt and hopelessness have broken wide open! Can you identify with him, though? Do any of Moses' words strike a familiar chord with you and your struggles in life? We, like Moses, too often take our eyes off God's ability, and rather focus on our inability to meet the challenges of the day.

God gave an answer to Moses, though it may not have been quite the answer that Moses wanted to hear. "Tell the people: 'Consecrate yourselves in preparation for tomorrow, when you will eat meat…now the Lord will give you meat, and you will eat it. You will not eat it for just one day, or two days, or five, ten or twenty days, but for a whole month – until it comes out of your nostrils and you loathe it – because you have rejected the Lord, who is among you, and have wailed before Him, saying, "Why did we ever leave Egypt?"' (Numbers 11:18-20) Do you get the feeling that God might be annoyed with His people right about now? It would be about this time that I might be trying to find a dark corner to hide in. Moses keeps on questioning God's ability. He replies to God, "Here I am among six hundred thousand men on foot, and You say, 'I will give them meat to eat for a whole month!' Would they have enough if flocks and herds were slaughtered for them? Would they have enough if all the fish in the sea were caught for them? (Numbers 11:21-22) Bold words from Moses' mouth! Remember, too, that

Doubt – Hope's Saboteur

this was from a man who had witnessed the Lord providing manna to these same people day after day.

The Lord had a final answer for Moses. "Is the Lord's arm too short? You will now see whether or not what I say will come true for you…Now a wind went out from the Lord and drove quail in from the sea. It brought them down all around the camp to about three feet above the ground, as far as a day's walk in any direction. All that day and night and all the next day the people went out and gathered quail. No one gathered less than ten homers (about 60 bushels)." (Numbers 11:23, 31-32) What does that say about God's ability to answer our prayers, or about our doubts? God quelled Moses' doubts for the moment, but there was a price to pay for those doubts and the peoples' grumbling. God sent a plague which killed the people who had grumbled.

We see something similar in the New Testament with Jesus and His disciples. A tremendous crowd of people had followed Jesus after seeing all the miracles He had performed. Now the disciples are looking out over a sea of men, women and children with tired feet and empty bellies. Jesus decides to test Philip, one of His disciples. "Where shall we buy bread for these people to eat?" He asks Philip. Philip replies with an attitude of practicality and earthly limitation. "Eight months wages would not buy enough bread for each one to have a bite!" (John 6:7) He sees the people, and he sees limited resources. What he does not see, or is unwilling to see, is his Lord standing beside him, his

The God of Hope

Savior who is the source and supplier of all that he and the crowd would need. Peter's brother Andrew doesn't fare much better than Philip when assessing the situation through his own eyes of doubt. He notes, "Here is a boy with five small barley loaves and two small fish, but how far will they go among so many?" It's like Andrew is sitting on the fence, with faith on one side and doubt on the other. He's seen what Jesus can do, and it's almost like he offers the solution to the problem. These loaves and fish are something that Jesus can use to feed the crowd. But before he finishes his sentence, he is already letting doubt get the better of him…how far can these provisions go among so many? Doubt gets the upper hand once again!

If you had to think of one person in the Bible who was the quintessential doubter, who would it be? Of all the individuals in the Old and New Testaments, who is synonymous with a lack of faith? How about Thomas, one of Jesus disciples? Most people have heard of "doubting Thomas", right? Regardless of whether his doubt was greater than any of the other disciples, Thomas has and will continue to go down in history as <u>the</u> one who doubted. Whether that's a fair representation of Thomas or not, I can't say. We don't know too much about this disciple from the Bible. He certainly seemed to be loyal to Jesus, as he demonstrated around the time of Lazarus' death. Jesus had made the decision to return to Judea after learning that His friend Lazarus was sick. The disciples, however, were afraid because the last time Jesus had been there,

Doubt – Hope's Saboteur

the Jewish people had tried to stone Him. By extension, if the people of Judea wanted to kill Jesus, the rest of his disciples couldn't be all that safe accompanying Him. It was Thomas, though, who spoke up as a loyal follower…"Then Thomas said to the rest of the disciples, 'Let us also go, that we may die with Him.'" (John 11:16) Here was a man who was willing to die for Jesus. That's a pretty admirable trait. So how did this loyal disciple end up being known only for his doubting nature?

Shortly after Jesus rose from the dead, He appeared to the disciples…all of them, that is, except Thomas. When Thomas returned to the group, the rest of the disciples excitedly told him that they had seen the Lord. What was Thomas' reply to them? "Unless I see the nail marks in His hands and put my finger where the nails were, and put my hand into His side, I will not believe it." (John 20:25) Perhaps Thomas, being a pragmatist, had prepared himself for the worst, and didn't want to risk believing that something so miraculous as Jesus' resurrection could possibly be true. Regardless, he doubted. A week later, Jesus reappeared to the disciples, and this time Thomas was with them. Jesus had some tough words for His doubting disciple to hear. "Put your finger here; see My hands. Reach out your hand and put it in My side. Stop doubting and believe." (John 20:27) Thomas then finally responded with an affirmation of faith, "My Lord and my God!" (John 20:28), but Jesus had a stern response for Thomas. "Because you have seen Me, you have believed;

blessed are those who have not seen and yet have believed." (John 20:29)

Maybe Thomas gained this title of doubter because he was so vocal about his lack of faith. His statement to his fellow disciples was certainly a bold one. And to be fair, the rest of the disciples only believed that Jesus had risen from the dead when He appeared to them. In the sixteenth chapter of Mark, we read about the initial response of the disciples to Mary Magdalene when she informs them that Jesus is alive…they didn't believe it. Two other disciples also report meeting Jesus on the road, and the disciples didn't believe them either. Finally, Jesus appears directly to them, and then they believe. But He rebukes them "for their lack of faith and their stubborn refusal to believe those who had seen Him after He had risen." (Mark 16:14) Were they really any better than Thomas when it came to a level of faith? Probably not. Perhaps the lesson here is that we, like Thomas, should not boldly embrace our doubts where the Lord is concerned. The best advice we can receive is from the book of James in the New Testament…"But when he asks, he must believe and not doubt, because he who doubts is like a wave of the sea, blown and tossed by the wind. That man should not think that he will receive anything from the Lord; he is a double-minded man, unstable in all he does" (James 1:6-8).

If anyone could relate to doubt and being tossed by the wind and the waves, it would have been the disciples. Here again, when you think that your faith is not where it should be,

Doubt – Hope's Saboteur

you can get a little reassurance from the individuals who walked with Jesus and still doubted. These disciples were safe in Jesus' care when that storm threatened their boat. Instead of feeling protected by their Savior, all they could see were the crashing waves. Rather than resting in His promises, all they saw was someone who seemed so unconcerned as to be asleep while their lives were being threatened. The only thing they could say to their Lord was, "Teacher, don't you care if we drown?" Their own fears overshadowed any faith they could muster. Their doubt ruled the day, but Jesus was so much more than their doubts. With one command of "Quiet, be still", Jesus calmed the storm, although He may not have completed calmed his disciples' doubts. How are you doing in your boat? Are you in the middle of a storm, watching as the bottom of your boat fills with water, and the waves are getting higher and higher? Can you embrace the faith that Jesus called for in His disciples, or are you embracing your doubts?

What about one of Jesus' boldest disciples? Peter, the rock on which Christ's kingdom is built, demonstrated the grave consequences of even the most fleeting doubt. When Jesus goes out to meet the boat that the disciples are in, He walks on the water. When the disciples see Him approaching, they panic and assume that a ghost is coming for them. Peter, however, sees that it's Jesus. Ever the impulsive one, he jumps out of the boat and unbelievably starts walking on the water too. For that moment he forgets his doubt and fear, and faith rules the day. It's a faith which defies the laws of gravity. But in less than an instant, his faith begins to falter, and he suddenly starts to sink. He cries out to the Lord, who immediately grabs his hand and keeps him from going under, but the damage is done. The transition between faith and doubt happens in a few seconds. So I ask, "How is it with us today?" What hope could we have, what could we achieve if only we were able to keep the flame of faith lit for longer than a minute? Peter was there, he was actually walking on water. But just as quickly as he was flying he came crashing back down to earth. Just a second of doubt made all the difference, but it reaffirms what negative power doubt can have over a person. If faith as small as a mustard seed can move mountains, then doubt for only a second can sink ships (or disciples, as the case may be). Remember, God's word is pretty clear as it relates to doubt…he who doubts can expect to receive nothing from Him. We see evidence of that in Jesus' own hometown. Matthew thirteen describes the reaction Jesus' neighbors had to Him. They couldn't believe that someone they had known most of their lives could teach and do the things that He did. They probably thought, "Who does He think He is?" and were both skeptical of and offended by His claims. They believed there was no way this seemingly average citizen could be the Son of God. Jesus' response to them was straight and to the point. "Only in his hometown and in his own house is a prophet without honor." (Matthew 13:57) The Bible goes on to say that "He did not do many miracles there because of their lack of faith". Their doubt was the ultimate stumbling block to the miracles that faith could have produced. There's just no way around it...doubt can sabotage our best efforts at nurturing and maintaining hope.

How then do you hold fast to your faith when the winds of doubt come rushing into your life? You make sure that you are clothed with the armor of God. Ephesians six is the definitive chapter on how to defend oneself against the manipulative tactics of the devil and his insidious attacks of doubt. "Finally, be strong in the Lord and in His mighty power. Put on the full armor of God so that you can take your stand against the devil and his schemes...stand firm then with the belt of truth buckled around your waist, with the breastplate of righteousness in place, and with your feet fitted with the readiness that comes from the gospel of peace. In addition to all this, take up the shield of faith, with which you can extinguish all the flaming arrows of the evil one. Take the helmet of salvation and the sword of the Spirit, which is the Word of God. And pray in the Spirit on all occasions with all kinds of prayers and requests. (Eph. 6:10-18) Don't you just love the picture Ephesians paints of the battle defenses? Can't you envision each arrow the devil shoots at you as being deflected and neutralized by that shield of faith? There's an arrow of doubt, an arrow of despair, an arrow of hopelessness. They are all made ineffective when we protect ourselves with God's shield of faith!

The God of Hope

This description of the armor of God serves to reinforce the truth that evil is very much present in this world. With each passing year of my life I've come to realize that the devil is relentless in his efforts to bring God's children to the point of doubt and despair. When I was younger, it seemed overly dramatic to think in terms of a war between God and the devil. I knew that the devil existed according to my Sunday school lessons, but he seemed to exist in a more abstract form. When you're a child, the world has a lot fewer shades of gray in it. Things then were more black and white, and Satan and his tactics didn't quite register with my adolescent brain. Now, however, I realize that some of the devil's most effective tools are doubt and despair. Sometimes, of course, the devil will launch what I like to call an artillery attack against you. It's direct and fierce and you can feel it when it comes. Those are the days when you're car won't start, you've lost your cell phone, and your boss reams you out for something trivial. It's the days when so many bad things seem to happen at once that the devil's plan is easier to recognize. Those are the days when you can see the devil for what he is and can take steps to protect yourself accordingly. But more often it seems that Satan can be most successful when he launches a subtle but persistent "sneak attack" on you. Doubt and despair are the favorite weapons in his arsenal. What does despair feel like? It's a place where you feel completely without hope. You have no energy or motivation to live the life that God wants of you because life and its circumstances have sucked the faith right out of you. When someone tells you to hang on because there's light at the end of the tunnel, you're certain that the light is just the headlights of an oncoming train. At such a time of despair like that, how do you feel about God? Do you picture Him as a loving and merciful Father? Do you see Him as someone you want to spend time with each day? Or is He someone who has forsaken you and left you abandoned by the side of the road? Do you feel like having a relationship with someone that you feel has pushed you aside? That, my friend, is how the devil wears you down, stokes the flames of doubt, and robs you of hope.

I wish I could say that I was a person who never had any doubts about God and His promises. Most of all, I wish I didn't doubt His ability and willingness to provide me with the spiritual and material necessities of this life. Unfortunately, my sinful human nature leaves me sorely lacking in that regard. What gets particularly frustrating for me is that no matter how well God has provided for me in the past, I still look with perpetual uncertainty at His ability to provide for me in the future. Why is it so easy to doubt that He will be there for us tomorrow and so easy for us to forget that He was there for us yesterday?

Sometimes I wonder what it would have been like to be in the shoes of the early Israelites during the forty years they wandered in the desert. How did they look to the future with any degree of hope? There they were, basically wandering around in circles because of their rebellious attitude toward God. They

The God of Hope

lived a nomadic existence in the harsh desert, and had to depend on God for everything that they needed. God's instruction to His people was that He would provide food for them in the form of manna from heaven, but they were only to collect enough for one days' supply. If they collected any more than that, it would spoil. True to their reputation, some of the Israelites tried to hoard that manna, and sure enough, it spoiled. If I were in that situation, I think I would be very happy to get that day's supply of food at first. Being the person that I am, I would probably start thinking to myself, "Well, I know that God has provided for me today, but what if He decides to stop providing for me tomorrow?" Instead of just taking one day at a time and leaving the future in God's hands, I might be tempted to fast forward to the future. What if I get to day 2,812 and God suddenly stops providing? It wouldn't matter that God had provided manna for the previous 2,811 days; my doubts would still have me wondering what was going to happen the following day.

As much as I have struggled with doubt, the one thing I've realized as I get older is that doubt is a choice. Although my personality may predispose me to doubt God's faithfulness, it's ultimately my decision whether I take God at His word, or let my fears and doubts get the better of me. When those doubts attack me, it's my choice as to whether I direct my thoughts to examples of God's previous faithfulness or whether I allow myself to be overcome by the prospects of that hopeless future. In that sense, the best advice is to focus on the words of

Doubt – Hope's Saboteur

Philippians 4:8. "Finally brothers, whatever is true, whatever is noble, whatever is lovely, whatever is admirable – if anything is excellent or praiseworthy – think about such things." Don't entertain, for even a moment, any thought that would plant the seed of doubt in your mind. You may soon find yourself going under like Peter did. I'll admit there is a fine line that exists between faith and doubt, and sometimes it doesn't take much to tip the scale in favor of doubt. But consider how the world might be very different if the heroes of faith in the Bible had given in to their doubts and fears. Joseph would never have reached a position of authority where he became instrumental in saving his family from starvation. Moses might never have had the courage to stand before Pharaoh demanding the Israelites' release from slavery. The Israelite nation would certainly have reached the Promised Land that much sooner had they not fallen prey to the doubts of their ten fearful spies. David might have given up ever waiting to be king after having faced Saul's attacks against him. Gideon would never have stood firm when facing an enemy force much greater than his own. The disciples would have hidden from their persecutors rather than boldly proclaiming the life saving message of their resurrected Lord!

The truth about doubt is this. If we look at our lives based primarily on an earthly perspective, doubt is sure to be our constant companion. Living life without focusing our eyes on God and His promises is a sure fire way to lose hope. Such an existence guarantees that our daily struggles will paralyze us and

The God of Hope

prevent us from moving forward along the path and purpose that God has set out for us. The path before us may at times be dark and uncertain, but we should not allow ourselves to be misdirected by our doubts. Never forget that as Christians, we "walk by faith, not by sight". Doubt has no place on the road to hope. We can overcome doubt when we heed the advice of Paul in his letter to the Philippians. "Forgetting what is behind and straining toward what is ahead, I press on toward the goal to win the prize for which God has called me heavenward in Christ Jesus." (Philippians 3:13-14) There is no greater comfort than to know that the ultimate destination of our struggle of faith is eternity with Christ. On those days when doubt threatens to steal your peace and hope, be like the struggling father begging on behalf of his child and cry out to the Lord, "I believe; help my unbelief!

Chapter 9

HOPE DEFERRED

How long, O Lord? Will You forget me forever?
Psalm 13:1

Hope deferred makes the heart sick, but a longing fulfilled is a
tree of life
Proverbs 13:12

The previous chapters of this book have focused mainly on the hope that God can provide during the challenging times in one's life. What happens to your outlook on life and your entire belief system, though, when God is silent? What do you do when you've kept the faith, prayed without ceasing, and trusted God to bring you relief in one form or another, but there is no answer from Him? What then?

A person's response to trying times is often influenced by two main factors. The first is the severity of the trial, and the second is how long each trial lasts. Facing a single hardship or challenge over a short period of time may seem like something we can endure. Add to that one or more problems (such as marital, health, or financial troubles), and have those problems drag on for a much longer period of time, and suddenly our

The God of Hope

ability to handle things on our own becomes a much tougher job. The end result of those struggles may have us doubting God's ability to help us. Nothing brings about true hopelessness faster than considering the possibility that God cannot or will not help us when we cry out to Him.

Are you familiar with the five stages of grief? After the loss of a loved one, the process of grieving for that person is often described as occurring in five stages. These stages are defined as denial, anger, bargaining, depression and finally acceptance. The path to hopelessness is also a process: it doesn't take place all at once. In a lot of ways, I think it bears many similarities to the stages of grief. It can be an insidious process, one where you don't even realize you've reached hopelessness until you're tightly in its grip.

The road to hopelessness often starts with negative circumstances that are usually beyond our control. In this world we're taught that self sufficiency is a good thing, and that being the master of our universe is a worthy goal. For certain aspects of our life I suppose that's okay. But when self sufficiency begins to interfere with our relationship with God, we're headed down a road that leads us farther away from Him. We look to create our own future, our own success, and foolishly our own hope in this world. Ultimately, our plans get turned upside down because no one in this world can completely control the circumstances around them. We make plans and God laughs, or so the saying goes. Perhaps we just don't want to admit that we

Hope Deferred

aren't in control. We are, in effect, denying the sovereignty of God and His critical role in the events of our life. We don't want to admit that He knows better than we do. So what happens when we have our life all mapped out and then something happens to derail those plans? The boat we're in is getting harder to keep on course, so we hold on tighter to the rudder and use all of our strength to keep the boat heading in the direction we've decided is best. But perhaps God wants you sailing in a different direction. Despite knowing intellectually that "in all things God works for the good of those who love Him", you're not feeling too confident in God's ability to do right by you. That leads to the second stage of hopelessness...anger.

It's a perfectly human response to get angry when things don't go the way we want them to. Part of that may be because we're inherently selfish beings, but part of it may be that unplanned life events have a way of amplifying the uncertainties of life. Pain, suffering and other challenges reinforce the life lesson that our days are unpredictable. The older we get, the more we, as Christians, realize that we're at the mercy of a God we hope is as compassionate and gracious as the Bible says He is. Many books have been written trying to explain why bad things happen to good people. Yes, the world is plagued by original sin, and no one is immune from the effects of Adam and Eve's actions in the Garden of Eden. It can be a difficult thing accepting the illness or tragedy that God may allow into our lives. So perhaps you start to get angry with God. You ask yourself, "Why is this happening to me? I'm trying to live a life that pleases God. I don't lie, cheat or steal. I try to help my fellow man, and all I get is grief and heartache." Your resentment grows, because you have enough belief and faith to know that God has something to do with how the events in your life unfold. Faith tells us that God can intervene on our behalf in whatever circumstances we may be facing. Anger comes when, for reasons unknown to us, God has chosen not to intervene on our behalf. Where's the compassion and mercy in that? Why would God *not* help us? Why do the wicked people in the world seem to prosper, while the good people seem to have such a tough time of things? Your study of God's word doesn't yield the answers you're looking for. You turn to the Psalms, usually a reliable source of comfort in times of trial, but even they provide little consolation. Still God remains silent. You realize your anger brings you no relief, so you're now at the third stage of your journey…bargaining.

You've cried out to God and He's remaining silent, so you figure you must be doing something wrong, but you don't know what that is. So you tell Him if He helps you, you will devote yourself to being a better person and better Christian. In essence, you're trying to make a deal with God to end your suffering or protect you from harm. Legend has it that Martin Luther, one of the central figures in the Protestant reformation, changed the course of his life and career after a sudden crisis in his youth. On his way back to the University of Erfurt to continue his law studies, young Martin encountered a severe thunderstorm. Lightning struck so close to him that he was thrown to the ground. In his fear, he is said to have called out "Help me St. Anne, I will become a monk!" Under that extreme duress, Martin's fear-driven response was to bargain with God for his life, while using St. Anne as an intermediary. To his credit, having survived that terrifying experience, he followed through on his end of the bargain. He ended his study of law and instead entered an Augustinian monastery. While our bargaining with God may not be so dramatic, it's still one of the tools we use to bend God to our will, rather than to submit to His. More often than not, our best attempts at bargaining fail, and God remains silent still.

It may be at this point when you realize that nothing you do will change the circumstances around you. Be it health problems, financial or relationship trouble, you realize just how powerless you are to affect meaningful change in your life. It's that acknowledgement of the lack of control that can be paralyzing. You feel you have truly come to the end of your rope. A deep depression has settled over you. For perhaps the first time you seriously entertain the thought that things won't ever get better.

Psychologist Martin Seligman conducted a fascinating series of experiments in the nineteen sixties and seventies. He wanted to see how groups of dogs responded to certain negative stimuli…in this case, electrical shocks. The dogs in one group would receive electrical shocks but were able to escape the shocks by jumping into an adjacent area of their enclosure. The dogs in a second group also experienced electrical shocks, but these dogs were prevented from escaping the shocks. This group had to endure with no relief. After awhile, this second group accepted the shocks and just lay there taking it. Even after the experiment was modified so that these dogs could now escape the shock, they chose to just lay motionless and not try to escape. They didn't try to move even though they now could. Seligman described the results of his experiment as "learned helplessness". As an animal lover, I have a serious problem with how this experiment was carried out, but its results are powerful and the findings have been correlated to similar responses in people. Can you relate to what the dogs experienced? How many people, after enduring years of struggles with no relief in sight, mentally shut down? They get to the point where they feel life isn't worth the effort anymore. They become spiritual and emotional zombies, surviving each day but not realizing or embracing the dreams that God still has for them. To them, there is no hope and there never will be. They're convinced that God doesn't hear and will never answer them. They have hit rock bottom.

If it's true that when we hit rock bottom, there's no place to look but up, then we have reached the final stage of hopelessness…acceptance. If there truly is a divine purpose to suffering, then this is the stage where we find it. Because if you have weathered the storms and have reached this point, the most important lesson to be learned is that we truly are powerless, but God is not. We're not in control of our lives, but God is. He has a purpose for every bit of pain and suffering in life. The book of First Peter helps to shed light on suffering, embracing the eternal perspective. "Praise be to the God and Father of our Lord Jesus Christ. In His great mercy He has given us new birth into a living hope through the resurrection of Jesus Christ from the dead, and into an inheritance that can never perish, spoil or fade – kept in heaven for you, who through faith are shielded by God's power until the coming of the salvation that is ready to be revealed in the last time. In this you greatly rejoice, though now for a little while you may have had to suffer grief in all kinds of trials. These have come so that your faith – of greater worth than gold, which perishes even though refined by fire – may be proved genuine and may result in praise, glory and honor when Jesus Christ is revealed." (1 Peter 1:3-7). It's exactly because of the sacrificial death of Jesus Christ and what it has done for us that we're able to hold onto hope in the face of a seemingly hopeless existence. Whatever God allows into your life is there to bring you closer to Him, to strengthen your faith in His sovereignty and to accept His place in your life. We can look at ourselves as the human equivalent of diamonds in the making. Diamonds start out as very ordinary carbon. It's only through long term exposure to tremendous heat and pressure that carbon is changed into a precious gem. As harsh as the process of metamorphosis is, in the end it produces something of much greater worth than when the process started. Gold is refined through exposure to fiery temperatures. For us, the test is whether or not we can accept God's will through the refining process. Even harder still, can we, like Peter, be willing to bring praise, honor and glory through and in spite of the refining process?

The band Casting Crowns came out with a song several years ago that speaks to this very issue. Band member and songwriter Mark Hall wrote the song, "Praise You in This Storm" after getting to know a young cancer patient and her family. Seeing what the family went through and how they coped with the child's illness inspired Mark to speak to the question of how believers could still praise God in the midst of suffering. The lyrics speak to the initial belief that God would come through and answer the prayers of the faithful Christian in a way that reaffirms belief in a loving God. Over time it becomes clear that favorable answers to prayer are not to be had. Admitting that God is still faithful despite seeming unanswered prayers can be difficult but necessary when our hope is deferred. Shortly after this song was introduced on the radio, hurricane Katrina hit, and the song found an audience in a whole new group of people facing seemingly insurmountable challenges. Although Mark Hall originally wrote the song for someone else, the song took on new meaning for him and his wife when their newly adopted daughter suffered serious medical issues. This one song was able to strike a chord with many hurting

Hope Deferred

Christians, with its' valuable message of learning to praise God in the midst of life's storms.

While it's true that no one but you and God can know just how bad a place you may be at right now, the truth is that we are all alike in our daily struggles. Some individuals may be facing financial struggles, others serious health issues. Your marriage or relationship may be at a crossroads, or your children may be heading in a direction that defies your best efforts at parental guidance. While it may seem that some lives have it easier than others, the truth is that no one living on this earth gets through it without pain and suffering. It has been this way since the fall of man in the Garden of Eden, and that won't change until the Lord returns. If misery loves company, it may be comforting to know that those in the Bible shared the same, if not worse, hardships than we face today.

Consider the case of poor Noah. By all accounts, Noah was a righteous man. He was described as blameless among the people of his time, and was known to walk with God. Because of the corruption and violence of the world around him, God condemned all living things on the face of the earth to be destroyed by a great flood. For six hundred years Noah had lived on the earth, and had probably grown accustomed to life as it was. Can you imagine what he must have thought when God told him that the earth was going to be destroyed? There had to be fear and uncertainty in response to this news, maybe even a little sense of hopelessness. Regardless of what Noah might have been feeling at the time, he faithfully followed God's instructions to build an ark to house his family and the animals that God had chosen to survive the flood. When God directed him to do so, Noah loaded his family and all those animals up in the ark. More than likely he did this in the presence of his mocking neighbors. Then Noah and his small family waited for the rain to come. When it finally did, it didn't stop raining for forty days and forty nights. So much rain fell that the entire surface of the earth was under water. Imagine the thoughts running through Noah's head while living in that ark. Everything that he and his family had known was gone…completely destroyed. For one hundred fifty days the waters flooded the earth. How must it have felt to be bottled up in an ark with nothing but water and desolation around you? Even though the rain eventually stopped, Noah and his family weren't able to leave the ark for another extended period of time. By all estimations, Noah and his family spent over a year in that ark from the time the rain started to the time the waters had receded enough for his family and the animals to exit. Certainly Noah's hopes for the future had to be shaken at least a little. What do you do when the only world you have known has been taken from you? Noah did the one thing he could do…he hung on and clung to the One who had saved him from the flood. God had protected Noah and his family through the rains, and now He blessed them with a new life and covenant. Although Noah had lost his former life, he still had all he needed to survive…he had the Lord.

Hope Deferred

Then there was Moses…again. Having been raised by Pharaoh's daughter, Moses' early life was one of great privilege…quite unlike what his fellow Israelites experienced as slaves in Egypt. His lifestyle changed dramatically when God's plan for him began to unfold. Moses went from honored among Pharaoh's family to a fugitive on the run. A new life of hardship and uncertainty was waiting for him. It was at Horeb that God made His plan for Moses known to him. Nothing about that plan sounded easy. In fact, Moses looked for any excuse to escape the path that God had laid out for him. He wanted no part of leading the Israelites out of Egypt, and told God just as much. Finally, Moses realized that there was no way of avoiding what God had called him to do. Despite his misgivings, he approached Pharaoh with God's plan. The only problem was that Pharaoh had a different plan for the people of Israel. There Moses was…stuck between a rock and a hard place. God had told him what to do but Pharaoh wasn't cooperating. Instead of consenting to Moses' request to let the Israelites go, Pharaoh responded by increasing the workload on them. Now Moses not only had to deal with Pharaoh, but also with his own people, who blamed him for their new found hardships. His plea before God expressed his frustration with the situation. "O Lord, why have You brought trouble upon this people? Is this why You sent me? Ever since I went to Pharaoh to speak in Your name, he has brought trouble upon this people, and You have not rescued Your people at all." (Exodus 5:22-23) Can you sense a bit of resentment in Moses' words? Moses must have wondered why God was making things so difficult for him. If God really wanted His people to be free from slavery, why didn't He just make things easier? Despite the initial rebuttal, God sent Moses back to the Egyptian ruler a second time. You see, God had hardened Pharaoh's heart so that Moses could not sway him. God unleashed plague after plague on the Egyptians, and still Pharaoh wouldn't give in and release the Israelites. When Pharaoh finally consented to their release, it wasn't too long before he changed his mind and sent his army to chase after them. Things certainly weren't getting any easier for Moses, were they? In the end, God rescued Moses and the Israelites from the Egyptians, but Moses would have to suffer through leading a rebellious people in the desert for forty years. His life was probably a lot different from what he imagined it would be. I suspect Moses faced many a day where his hope in the Lord must have wavered.

If ever there was a person in the Bible who had a rough time of things, though, it was Job. Things didn't start out that way for this righteous man of God. At first glance, it seemed that his life was blessed. The first chapter of the book named after him described him this way. "He had seven sons and three daughters, and he owned seven thousand sheep, three thousand camels, five hundred yoke of oxen and five hundred donkeys, and had a large number of servants. He was the greatest man among all the people of the East." (Job 1:1-3). This was quite the description of a man who seemingly had it all. As we learned a little earlier, things changed suddenly for this man and his family. In a short span of time, Job found that his children and servants had all been killed, and his livestock had been stolen or destroyed. He is left with nothing, yet he doesn't curse God. In fact, his response to all of this sudden tragedy is one of the most profound statements of faith… "The Lord gave and the Lord hath taken away; blessed be the name of the Lord." (Job 1:21, KJV).

When those tremendous losses were followed by a painful skin disease, and his wife and friends offer no support, Job refuses to relinquish his hope in the Lord. Of course, he was correct in his response. He did maintain his steadfastness throughout these trials, and the Lord delivered him. In fact, the final chapter of Job records that "the Lord made him prosperous again and gave him twice as much as he had before…the Lord blessed the latter part of Job's life more than the first." (Job 42:10, 12).

Whenever I read through the account of Job's sufferings, there are a few things that bother me. The first involves the affliction of someone who was clearly a righteous man. It comes down once again to that age old question of why bad things happen to good people. Intellectually, I understand that the tragedies and trials of life are not only reserved for people that "deserve" them. Look around and you'll see plenty of good people who are struck down for no seemingly good reason. One has only to think of tragic events like natural disasters and terrorist attacks to realize that horrible things happen to innocent people…casualties of nature's fury and senseless acts of violence. Lives are forever changed by the loss of loved ones and grievous injuries suffered. Did any of those people deserve what happened to them? We would say no, of course not. Still, God allows these things to happen. We ask why, and begin to question whether God could possibly love us if He apparently does nothing to prevent such tragedy.

What perhaps bothers me most about the story of Job is why Job had to go through this ordeal in the first place. In all honesty, I'm particularly unsettled by the fact that Job's suffering was the result of what was essentially a bet between God and Satan. This may be dangerous ground to tread, but I question why God would allow a "contest" to dictate Job's fate. Had Job known what was going on behind the scenes, what had precipitated this series of assaults on him, would he have responded differently? Maybe not, but the thought of wagering on the degree of a person's faithfulness in suffering seems almost too much to bear.

To make matters worse, some of Job's well meaning, but nonetheless misguided friends, believed that Job was suffering his fate because of some unconfessed sin in his life. Although this wasn't the case, the not knowing why he was experiencing these painful trials only worsened Job's despair. Have you ever wondered how you would respond if faced with similar circumstances as Job? Perhaps you have experienced some of the heartache and tragedy that he faced. Maybe right now you're in the middle of a trial that God is using to demonstrate His authority in your life. At the moment it may seem like a hard pill to swallow. If you have a few friends like Job had, that pill may have a particularly bitter taste to it. In the midst of all that suffering, how long can you hang on?

I've often wondered how long Job had to suffer through all the trials that God sent him. From the Biblical description, the loss of Job's children and possessions came pretty quickly. The grieving process most certainly lasted a long time. As for the physical suffering though, how long did he have to endure that? Perhaps that shouldn't matter, but human nature being what it is, I ask myself that question because it seems so relevant to a person's ability to maintain hope. When you're going through a particularly dark period in your life, one of the coping mechanisms you might use is reassuring yourself that tough times don't last forever. Have you ever had someone say to you, "This too, shall pass"? Eventually things in your life will improve, right? You convince yourself that you can hang on until the storm has passed and the clouds have cleared. For a while you do hang on. Then days turn into weeks, which turn into months, and you start to wonder how much longer you can hold on. You're clinging to God and His promises, but all you're getting from God is that deafening silence. You read your Bible, especially all those verses pertaining to your situation and you remind yourself of Job, and David, and St. Paul, and all those heroes of faith that fought the good fight. The only problem is that you don't feel very strong or heroic. That slight glimmer of hope for a better tomorrow is fading fast. You wonder, how long before the sky clears? Or worse yet, what if the sky never clears? What happens if this is the way things are going to be for the rest of your life? Suddenly you're hit with a wave of spiritual exhaustion and despair. You wonder if it's even worth trying anymore, and soon you find yourself echoing the words of the psalmist, "How long, O Lord? Will You forget me forever?" (Psalm 13:1)

Do you beat up on yourself because you're not willing to accept the difficulties God has allowed in your life? If so, you need to consider the one person on this earth who was without sin. Jesus was the perfect Son of God and yet demonstrated some of the same raw human emotions that we feel when we encounter hardship. Somehow I feel that even though Jesus became flesh and blood like the rest of us, He was somehow immune to the suffering that we all face because of His status as God's Son. Certainly, Jesus knew it was His Father's will that He would have to die for the sins of the fallen world. He told His disciples that this would be His fate. After all, that was His purpose on this earth. In the Garden of Gethsemane, Jesus experienced all the pain one would expect who was facing what He had to face. "My soul is overwhelmed with sorrow to the point of death", He told the disciples with Him (Matthew 26: 38). When He was by Himself, He fell to the ground and prayed,

Hope Deferred

"My Father, if it is possible, may this cup be taken from Me. Yet not as I will, but as You will" (Matthew 26:39). Here was the Son of God praying for relief and a means of escape from what the future held for Him. But even as He prayed for relief, He clearly acknowledged that He was submitting Himself to the will of God. Finally, when He was hanging on the cross, He cried out to His Father, "My God, my God, why have You forsaken Me?" (Matthew 27:46) If even Jesus could feel that His Father had abandoned Him, is it any wonder that we often feel that God has abandoned us as well? However strong those feelings of abandonment may be, we need to hold on to the Biblical truths, to God's promises that He will never leave us on forsake us.

One of my all time favorite movies is the classic Christmas tale, "A Christmas Story". I know, I know, when people think of their favorite Christmas movie, it's usually "It's a Wonderful Life" or "White Christmas". But "A Christmas Story" is a wonderful little account of a boy's hope and the expectations and disappointments associated with it. Young Ralphie Parker, the main character, has one thing on his mind as Christmas approaches…getting a Red Ryder BB gun. Never mind that virtually all of the adults around him are trying to persuade him to give up his dream of owning the best present a boy his age could imagine. His mother, his teacher, even Santa and the elves at the local department store, all warn him of the dangers of owning the gun. They try to discourage him with visions of self-inflicted ocular trauma. Undeterred, young

The God of Hope

Ralphie hatches imaginative schemes to make his dream come true…leaving obvious clues for his parents and getting in Santa's good graces. As Christmas fast approaches, Ralphie is certain that a Red Ryder BB gun will be waiting for him under the tree. Hope really does spring eternal for him, and he's relentless in his efforts. But all of his planning and hoping seem fruitless, when even the "big guy", Santa, informs him of the dangers of his longed for Red Ryder. As his parents pick him up from Santa's station, his father can't help but see the look of dejection on his oldest son's face. He asks his son if he told Santa what he wanted for Christmas, and if he has been a good boy. Ralphie answers unenthusiastically, and his father tries to encourage him by reassuring him that Santa always knows. Finally, the much anticipated day arrives, the one our hero Ralphie has been waiting for all year. He and his brother tear open their presents in rapid succession. After the wrapping paper is strewn all over the floor and all the presents have been opened, Ralphie realizes that there is no Red Ryder. The one thing he has been hoping for never materializes. All his efforts and his undying hope have resulted in nothing but disappointment. At this point, it seems that all hope is lost for his dream of owning the best BB gun in town. He feels like he has been betrayed. Yet all the while his father has seen the longing of his son's heart. When Ralphie's hope has been all but extinguished with the last present, and he has suffered the humiliation of lesser presents like a pink bunny suit, Ralphie has experienced the ultimate heartbreak of a boy his age. Then at the very last moment, his father directs him to one last package hidden away in the corner. Ralphie dare not rekindle any hope, lest he be disappointed again. At his father's urging, he retrieves the package, and with mounting excitement, unwraps it to discover that he's holding the precious Red Ryder in his hands. His father knew all along what his heart desired, even reassured him that Santa knew his wishes. Even when it all seemed hopeless, events were happening behind the scenes that were orchestrating the fulfillment of Ralphie's heartfelt dream. Although it's just a movie, it strikes a chord with me. We, like Ralphie, are often childlike in our view of the world. When we hope for something, at first we have a positive attitude that that hope will be fulfilled. At least for a while, we can maintain that optimism. As time drags on and our hopes aren't met, it gets harder and harder to stay positive. When all the presents are opened and we're still left empty handed, we have all but given up on God playing a meaningful role in our lives. But just like Ralphie's father in the movie, who reassured him that Santa knew what he longed for, we can be reassured that our heavenly Father knows the deepest desires of our heart and is orchestrating circumstances in our lives so that all things will work for our good.

Despite your present circumstances, however despairing they may be, can you trust that your heavenly Father has not forgotten you? That He knows what you need and the exact time that you need it? Can you take comfort in the certainty that God is more reliable than even the best of earthly fathers? Jesus compared earthly fathers to our one true heavenly Father. "Which of you, if his son asked for bread, will give him a stone? Or if he asks for a fish, will give him a snake? If you, then, though you are evil, know how to give good gifts to your children, how much more will your Father in heaven give good gifts to those who ask Him! (Matthew 7:9-11). When you ask, and there is seeming silence, can you be reassured by the truth that "God knows what you need before you ask Him?" (Matthew 6:8). When there is no glimmer of hope in your life and no change in your dire circumstances, can you look to the One who offers the following reassurance? "Therefore we do not lose heart. Though outwardly we are wasting away, yet inwardly we are being renewed day by day. For our light and momentary troubles are achieving for us an eternal glory that far outweighs them all. So we fix our eyes not on what is seen, but on what is unseen. For what is seen is temporary, but what is unseen is eternal. (2 Corinthians 4:16-18) In the midst of your hardest trials, can you accept God's will for you in the moment? Harder still, can you keep your eyes fixed on Him when those trials don't seem to end? When earthly hope is fleeting, can you rest upon the promise of God's eternal hope?

Chapter 10

WAITING ON GOD

For in this hope we were saved. But hope that is seen is no hope at all. Who hopes for what they already have? But if we hope for what we do not yet have, we wait for it patiently.
Romans 8: 24, 25

We wait in hope for the Lord; He is our help and our shield.
Psalm 33: 20

Whatever the challenges and heartaches we may face in life, we have a choice in how we respond when God seems to be silent. We can choose to throw in the towel and give up completely on life, trying to forget our problems with anything that will distract us or numb our pain. We can choose to let our resentment and mounting anger over our situation get to a point where we decide that if God isn't going to help us, then we'll help ourselves. Or we can choose to hang on and wait for the Lord to come through. Most of us know what the Lord would want us to do, but when we've waited for so long and there's no relief in sight, it's easy to give up or take matters into our own hands.

The God of Hope

The easiest choice of the three when hard times come and stay is to just give up. It's the attitude that says there's no point trying to hang on anymore. Hope manages to elude regardless of what a person tries, so why try at all? It's that learned helplessness talked about in the last chapter. Too many people make this choice and allow their lives to spiral ever downward, harming themselves and their families with drugs, alcohol or other destructive addictions. They withdraw from society at all levels: physical, emotional and spiritual. It's a "hunker down" mentality, waiting for the storms in their life to pass by. The second choice requires more energy than the first, but oftentimes it's a combination of frustration, impatience and anger that motivates us to try to take control of our lives away from God. This world has known many a workaholic, who although admired by their peers for their work ethic, had spiritual lives that were non-existent or in ruins. These individuals think that if only they can work hard enough and earn enough money, things will improve and they will have the brighter future they're looking for. All the while they're running from the life that God has wanted to give them, the life without the burden of trying to create their own false hope. Unfortunately, they learn too late that when they try to find solutions that are outside of God's will, they have missed out on all that God had to offer.

Earth's first human inhabitants, Adam and Eve, had it all. They were residents of the Garden of Eden, a place of perfection. In this garden, there was no sin, and all of their needs were met by God. In fact, this first couple had pretty much free reign of the entire garden, with one noticeable exception. In the center of the garden, God had placed the tree of life and the tree of the knowledge of good and evil. Of all the restrictions God could have given to His children, He gave only one to Adam…"you are free to eat of any tree in the garden; but you must not eat from the tree of the knowledge of good and evil, for when you eat of it you will surely die." (Genesis 2:16-17) If it was you in the garden instead of Adam and Eve, do you think you would have been satisfied with the life that you had been given?

We don't know how long Adam and Eve had lived in the Garden before Satan launched his spiritual attack on them. What we do know is that Satan was very effective in convincing Eve that everything God had provided for her and Adam was still not enough. By the time Satan was through with Eve, she had bypassed God's most important directive and sought to satisfy her perceived needs on her own.

The devil is very good at his job. He will do whatever it takes to get you off the path of God's will and permanently chained to his spiritually bankrupt treadmill. The Bible gives a vivid description of this "author of lies". "Now the serpent was more crafty than any of the wild animals the Lord God had made. He said to the woman, "Did God *really* say, "You must not eat from any tree in the garden?" (Genesis 3:1) Brilliant, right? What did the devil do but plant the first seeds of doubt in Eve's mind…make her question what God had said. Now Satan had Eve right where he wanted her. He continued his subtle spiritual assault. "You will not surely die… for God knows that when you eat of it your eyes will be opened, and you will be like God, knowing good and evil." (Genesis 3:4-5) That was all it took for Eve to give in and turn her back on God. In one short moment Eve had gone from realizing the best that God had to offer, to beginning a new life of hardship and diminished hope. When confronted by God, Eve offered this short but painfully accurate confession…"The serpent deceived me, and I ate." (Genesis 3:13) She and Adam were living in paradise, with everything they could ever want. But the devil deceived them and convinced them it wasn't enough. Don't let Satan steal the only true hope that is of any value in your life… the hope provided by God through His son Jesus Christ.

  Consider Abraham, the father of the Israelite nation and a man who was faithful most of the time. In fact, it was that faith that was credited to him as righteousness. But even this righteous man didn't get it right all the time. God's promise that Abraham's descendants would be as numerous as the stars in the sky and the sand on the seashore sure sounded good, in spite of the fact that Abraham and his wife were old and had no children. God had given him the promise, and that was enough for him to maintain hope…at least for a while. After years of patiently waiting, however, that hope began to waver. Time went by and still no child, no heir to be the forerunner of the promised Israelite nation. So Abraham did what most of us tend to do when we don't get the answers from God we're waiting for. He began to doubt. Maybe God was wrong, maybe there really wasn't any hope for a family after all? Where did this trace of doubt lead Abraham? Did he hold on to God's promise and wait patiently, or did he try to work things out on his own? You can almost hear the words..."Well, if God isn't going to provide an heir for me, then maybe I need to take matters into my own hands." Ah, the first mistake in abandoning God's hope! What happened? Abraham slept with Sarah's maidservant Hagar, and Ishmael was born. Eventually, Sarah gave birth to Isaac, who *was* the fulfillment of God's original promise. But Abraham's abandonment of God's hope ultimately led to hatred between the two nations formed by Isaac and Ishmael. The consequence of Abraham's actions resulted in a rivalry between Isaac and Ishmael that has persisted throughout generations and created continued hardship among the nations of the world to this day. Can you imagine how the world today might be different, if only Abraham had not doubted God and circumvented His will?

What of Samson, a man of incredible God-given strength who lived during the period of the Old Testament judges? His life was one where God had set out the roadmap for this future leader of Israel, but Samson decided that he would rather travel his own path.

The God of Hope

Once again the Israelites had rebelled against God and were suffering the consequences. God had allowed their rivals, the Philistines, to oppress them for forty years. Despite the continued disobedience of His children, God was orchestrating events that would lead to their deliverance. An angel of the Lord appeared to the parents of the yet unborn Samson, and told them that they would soon have a son who was to be set apart to God from birth, and who would begin to rescue Israel from the Philistines. Samson was that son.

As Samson grew, the Bible says that the Lord blessed him and filled him with the Spirit. While he was set apart to do the Lord's work and had incredible strength, he also had some serious weaknesses. He had issues with pride and anger, and he definitely had a weakness toward the opposite sex. A short-lived marriage to a Philistine woman fueled his anger and need for revenge. His actions escalated hostilities with the Philistines, and they were determined to destroy him. None of that seemed to bother Samson, though. For twenty years he fought against the Philistines, and the Lord remained with him. Eventually, his own pride led to his downfall. Samson met and fell in love with Delilah, who was more than willing to broker a deal with the Philistines to uncover the source of Samson's strength. Time after time Delilah pleaded with Samson to divulge his secret. If you read the account in the sixteenth chapter of Judges, it seems as if Samson is playing a game with his girlfriend. He acts like it's all one big joke. Finally, after much crying and manipulation,

Waiting on God

Delilah wears Samson down and he reveals that it's his long hair that is the source of his strength. Shortly after that, Delilah lulls him to sleep and then gets the local barber to shave off Samson's hair. His strength is now gone.

Delilah collects her money from the Philistines. Summoning her best acting skills, she wakes Samson with a warning that the Philistines are upon him. Samson opens his eyes and expects to defeat his attackers as before. But this is literally a rude awakening for him. He doesn't realize that his strength and the Lord have left him. In short order the Philistines subdue him. For the first time, Samson knows what it's like to live life without the Lord. He's learning a hard lesson about what it means to go his own way. The Philistines blind him and throw him into prison. So much for the man with superhuman strength.

Samson may not have been the greatest when it came to waiting on God. Physical invincibility might be considered a tremendous asset, but I suspect it also might be considered a liability if it leads you to believe that you can handle life on your own. I wonder if Samson spent time in that prison reflecting on how he might have handled things differently in his life. Although his actions had brought him to that prison, God had not abandoned him. While Samson was learning what it meant to wait on God, something else was happening…his hair was growing back. The Philistines were confident that Samson was no longer a problem, but they had forgotten about that hair! As they were celebrating and praising their false god for delivering

The God of Hope

Samson into their hands, they had him brought out of prison to entertain them. In the midst of all his enemies, Samson uttered a final prayer to the Lord. "O Sovereign Lord, remember me. O God, please strengthen me just once more, and let me with one blow get revenge on the Philistines for my two eyes." (Judges 16:28) God heard Samson's prayer and granted his request. With one last show of strength, he caused the Philistine temple to come crashing down on all the people, killing them and him. Did his life have to end that way? Had he followed God's path more closely, would things have been different for him? He had been chosen by God to deliver the Israelites from the Philistines, and he certainly did that. It just seems like a life cut short because he followed his own lead rather than God's.

Then there were the brothers Aaron and Moses. Both were instrumental in God's plan to lead the Israelite nation out of captivity. Yet both of these men individually made decisions that defied God's instructions. Aaron, Moses' big brother, was left at the foot of Mount Sinai when Moses went to receive the Ten Commandments from the Lord. It wasn't long before the rebellious Israelites started complaining to Aaron that Moses was taking too long up on that mountain. In short order Aaron decided the appropriate course of action was to fashion a golden calf to worship. After all God had done for the Israelites, they and Aaron quickly abandoned the Lord for a lifeless object that they credited with freeing them. Because Aaron was so willing

Waiting on God

to turn his back on God and lead the people astray, many Israelites lost their lives.

Some time later, these two men were denied entry into the Promised Land because they decided to do things their way instead of God's way. Camped out in the desert with no water, the nation of Israel was doing what they did best...grumbling and complaining. Exasperated, Moses and his brother Aaron at first did the right thing...they asked the Lord for help. God responded by instructing Moses to take his staff and speak to a rock, so that water would flow from the rock, allowing the people and their livestock to drink. But Moses was frustrated by the grumbling of the people and he decided to ignore God's instructions. Perhaps he felt that speaking to the rock wouldn't do the trick, so he struck the rock with his staff instead. God still allowed the water to flow from the rock, but He had some harsh words for Moses and his accomplice brother. "Because you did not trust in Me enough to honor Me as holy in the sight of the Israelites, you will not bring this community into the land I give them." (Numbers 20:12) That was that. Moses, who had borne the burden of leading this wayward nation for so many years, was that close to reaching the Promised Land. Had he just done what the Lord had told him to do, his feet would have touched the land that was flowing with milk and honey. Instead, he forfeited all the blessing that God had waiting for him because he chose his own way over God's!

The God of Hope

If Moses and Aaron, the chosen leaders of the Israelites, had a hard time submitting to God's will, imagine how difficult it must have been for the whole Israelite nation. For this people headed to the Promised Land, they just wanted a life better than what they had had as slaves in Egypt. When the Lord told them He would lead them out of Egypt to freedom, it must have sounded too good to be true. Those words represented the fulfillment of all their hopes. After they were free and the Egyptian army had been destroyed, it wasn't long before they started complaining. They complained that there wasn't any food to eat, so God provided them with manna. Then they were tired of manna, so God provided quail. Each time the Lord heard their complaints, He patiently and mercifully provided a solution for them. They still complained. "It would have been better for us never to have left Egypt than to die in the desert", they moaned. Through all of this grumbling, God's plan never changed. The hope that He had given to His people had not disappeared. From God's perspective, the goal *was* for His people to reach the Promised Land. In fact, in two years He had brought them to the outskirts of Canaan. The Israelites were so close to the fulfillment of that hope, but instead of accepting what God was providing for them, they laid obstacles in their own way. Instead of taking God at His word, they entertained doubts in their own minds and reasons why they couldn't obtain what God was willing to give them. Twelve Israelite spies were sent out to explore the land and see if it was all it was cracked up to be. In truth, it was a land flowing with milk and honey, just as the Lord had said. But only two of the twelve spies, Caleb and Joshua, took God at His word and believed that the fulfillment of hope was within their reach. The other ten spies reported back that the city was highly fortified and the people there were giants. That may have been true, but how quickly they had forgotten what God had done for them in the past. If God could in one motion completely destroy the Egyptian army, taking care of the defenders of this new land would be easy work for Him. As a result, what should have taken two years took forty years instead. God declared that everyone twenty years or older, with the exception of Joshua and Caleb, would not enter the Promised Land. For their disbelief, they would be forced to wander in the desert until they had all died there. That doubting generation had lost out on the opportunity to live out the rest of their lives within God's generous provision because they weren't willing to trust that He knew best.

    In our own lives, are we so different from those doubting Israelites? How often do we sabotage the fulfillment of God's promises in our lives by deciding to fix our own problems rather than waiting on the Lord? How often is realization of what we hope for within our reach if only we would take God at His word? I must admit that I struggle with this more often than I would like. God has said that He would provide for all my needs, and yet each day I worry that tomorrow I won't have what I need to make ends meet. If I look back over all the years of my life, however, He has always provided for me. That provision may have come at the last moment, and the means to make those ends meet may have been more difficult than I would have liked, but He still met those needs. Even so, I let the world tell me that God isn't capable of doing what He says He will do. Can you relate to that? Your next door neighbor just lost his job, so you start to worry about what would happen if you lost yours? The economy still hasn't recovered after several years of a recession…what if it never recovers? What will you do? How will you pay the bills? Philippians 4: 6 states clearly that we should not be anxious about anything. Yet why are we so willing to take the word of a very unreliable world instead of the loving words of our heavenly Father? Why are we so good at sabotaging the peace that our Father wants to give us?

I'm still working out the reasons why it's so easy for people to rely on their own solutions rather than God's. I wish it were easier to trivialize all the concerns of this world by looking to the hope of an everlasting life. If we could do that, then the challenges and trials in this life wouldn't seem so overwhelming. Despite what we know in our heads from reading God's Word, the emotions of fear, doubt and confusion in our hearts are very real obstacles to holding onto the hope that God wants to provide. It ultimately comes down to a choice. Do we choose to believe what the world and its' so called life experts are telling us, or do we choose to take the more difficult path? Do we believe the One who tells us that despite the despair that the

Waiting on God

world wants to foster in us, the God of the universe knows each of us by name, and has promised us that He will never leave us or forsake us? Jesus told his disciples, "In this world you will have trouble. But take heart! I have overcome the world." (John 16:33) Can we hold onto that promise and wait on the Lord? Can we accept that God is in control of events and submit to His timing and plan, even if the road is long and the future uncertain?

David had been anointed king of Israel even while the nation's first king, Saul, still sat on the throne. But King Saul had turned his heart away from God. Although David was now God's first choice for king, he remained a political outcast for seven years, ducking and dodging Saul's attempts to assassinate him. Despite the promise from God, David lived in fear for his life every day of those many years. Multiple times he had the opportunity to take matters into his own hands and turn the tables on Saul. David could have killed Saul and then established himself as king. Instead, he decided to place himself in God's hands and wait on the Lord's timing. Eventually, Saul was killed in battle, and David became the legitimate ruler of Israel. Had he not waited, but instead done things his own way, he would have risked causing great division within the nation.

Another individual who can teach us a lot about waiting on the Lord is Joseph. Joseph was a young man of seventeen when his troubles started. It seemed he was the favorite son of his father Jacob, and his brothers were jealous of him. Of course

The God of Hope

it didn't help Joseph's cause when he flaunted his father's gifts to him, or described dreams to his brothers where they were bowing down in submission to him. His brothers decided that they were going to kill him. Had it not been for the intervention of Joseph's brother Reuben, he would have been killed. Instead, the brothers sold Joseph to a traveling caravan of merchants, who brought him to Egypt. Once there, Joseph was sold again to Potiphar, one of Pharaoh's officials. All of this must have been quite a shock to this young Israelite. Having led a privileged life as the favored son, he's now at the bottom of the food chain. He's in a foreign land, knows no one, and is facing an uncertain future. What does he do? He submits himself to the Lord's will. The Bible says that the Lord was with Joseph and he prospered in the house of Potiphar. He rose up the ranks until he was in charge of Potiphar's entire household. Finally, things seemed to have turned around for Joseph. Unfortunately his good fortune was short lived. Potiphar's wife had a wandering eye, and she tried to seduce Joseph. He refused her advances, at which point she falsely accused him of treachery, and Joseph suddenly found himself sitting in a prison cell. Any hope of a better life had again been shattered. Despite all of his troubles, he still chose to wait on the Lord. For two long years he sat in that prison, forgotten by a former prison mate he had helped. Finally the Lord intervened on Joseph's behalf. His prison mate eventually remembered him, and his talents were sought when none of Pharaoh's wise men could interpret the ruler's dreams. God gave

Waiting on God

Joseph the ability to do what no one else could, and as a result he went from prisoner to being put in charge of Pharaoh's palace. The span of time from Joseph being sold by his brothers to being put in charge of Pharaoh's affairs was thirteen long years. They were surely years filled with uncertainty and anxiety, but Joseph remained true to the Lord. He held on in the midst of trial and temptation, and the Lord made a way for him.

If you were to look at Joseph's life from his perspective, the trials that he encountered may have seemed pointless. It would be hard to imagine that what this young man had experienced would be used by God to bring about miraculous events in the future nation of Israel. But it was because of these struggles that Joseph eventually went on to become instrumental in saving his family from a terrible famine. Every circumstance was according to God's perfect timetable. From Jacob's standpoint, the famine in his country was a tremendous hardship, one that he would not have invited into his or his family's life. Yet, it was this very famine that ultimately led to the reunion with his son Joseph. Neither father nor son could possibly have envisioned how God would orchestrate events in their lives to achieve his desired results. What amazing things God can do in the lives of people who wait on Him!

Are you familiar with the story of Zerubbabel and the Jewish exiles? After king Nebuchadnezzar and the Babylonian army had conquered Jerusalem and destroyed the Lord's temple, most of the Jewish people were taken to Babylon as exiles.

The God of Hope

Everything these victims of war had known had been taken away from them...their homes, their security, their future. The holy temple, the epicenter of their Jewish faith, was completely and utterly destroyed. It must have appeared as if their entire way of life was gone forever. Surely they must have thought that they would never, as a people, be able to return home, especially considering the invincibility of the Babylonian empire. God had said there would be a seventy year exile for His people, and then they would return home to Jerusalem. Many must have died before Cyrus, king of Persia, issued the proclamation which finally allowed the Jews to return home. Of those who waited for so many years, it must have seemed like a dream come true when they headed back to their original promised land. When they returned home, however, the ruins of their previous life greeted them. There stood the rubble of the former temple, a grim reminder of the heartache and suffering they had experienced. In the end, they rebuilt the temple, but it took them many years of trouble and turmoil because of opposition from their enemies. Life may not have been as they remembered it, but finally God had brought them home and restored their hope.

Recall the bleeding woman and the invalid at the pool of Bethesda that we read about in chapter four. Both must have felt the hopelessness of waiting for healing that never seemed to come. This poor woman had tried everything with no success. Can you imagine the desperation she must have felt after all that time? Long before the days of medical insurance, she had spent all her money on doctors, hoping that they could cure her. Now, she had nothing left. While her health and her money may have been gone, she still had faith and some patience. After twelve long years of suffering, Jesus healed her. All the money and all the medical knowledge could not do what Jesus could do with a single touch. For this woman, waiting on Jesus had made all the difference. And what about that poor invalid who had suffered for thirty eight years? After watching all the others being healed instead of him, is it so hard to understand why he might have given way to bitterness and resentment at his lack of healing? Can you imagine how alone he must have felt, watching as every opportunity for a fresh start is snatched away from him? Each new day must have seemed as hopeless as the one before. But one day he encountered the Great Physician, and his life and health were renewed in an instant. Jesus said to him, "'Get up! Pick up your mat and walk.' At once the man was cured; he picked up his mat and walked." (John 5:8-9) After almost four long decades, his life was made new in more ways than one!

    Waiting on the Lord can be a difficult thing to do. God often doesn't provide for our needs or deliver us from a desperate situation right away. More often than not, God seems to wait until the last minute to provide. Have you ever felt that God answered your prayers like some of those suspense dramas on television? You know the ones…the hero of the show is staring at this huge bomb, and there are about fifty different colored wires that need to be cut in exactly the right sequence or else the bomb explodes. If you're really into the show you may even be screaming at the TV set, "Cut the wire!" There are twenty-three seconds left on the timer but the hero is calmly standing there. He's staring at that bomb, without a drop of sweat on him, while everyone else around him is ready to pass out. Then with two seconds on the clock he clips the right wire and the bomb is defused…crisis averted. Do you ever feel that God handles the crises in your life that way? You feel ready to collapse from the stress you're under, but God doesn't seem to be too concerned. When He finally does intervene, you want to be grateful, but your heart is beating like a freight train. In between twinges of panic you're muttering under your breath "Thanks a lot, but did you have to wait until the last minute?"

In my own life, I've found that God often takes things down to the wire before He helps me out. I'm not sure why this is the case…maybe He wants to see just how much I trust in His promises. I suspect that part of it may be God's way of stretching our faith and building perseverance in us so that we'll turn to Him in the future. It's just like the long distance runner, who near the end of his race may be thinking that he doesn't have the strength to finish. Somehow he holds on for just a little longer, building his stamina and by doing so finishes the race. In the spiritual sense, as God allows us to wait, we are strengthening our spiritual muscles and learning hard, but valuable, lessons along the way. In reading through the Bible, it seems this is true with many Old and New Testament individuals. Just why is it that God often waits until the last minute before He steps in and saves the day? He could intervene at any moment. Do you ever ask yourself why God's help never comes early?

Whether it be thirteen years for Joseph or thirty-eight years for a poolside invalid, the uncertainty as to if and when God will grant relief can be a burden on the soul. In the midst of suffering, time seems to pass at a snail's pace. A quote by one of the most intelligent men in recent history is especially accurate here. Albert Einstein, commenting on relativity, described it this way. "When you are courting a nice girl, an hour seems like a second. When you sit on a red hot cinder, a second seems like an hour. That's relativity." Isn't that so true? The good times in a person's life seem so short compared with how long the bad times seem to last.

Consider the situation the Israelites faced at the Red Sea. Finally free from Pharaoh and his army, there is open desert and the Promised Land ahead of them…until they realize that the Egyptian army is hot on their trail and a vast body of water is in front of them. They are no match for Pharaoh's military might and there are no ships to rescue them. They are trapped. They had to be wondering where God was and why He allowed them to be in this situation in the first place. Certainly God could have intervened on their behalf anywhere along the way to the Promised Land. He could have allowed Pharaoh to keep his word and let the Israelites leave Egypt without interference. Instead, Pharaoh changes his mind and sends his whole army to

The God of Hope

chase after them. God could have delayed the Egyptian army so that they didn't catch up to the fleeing Israelites. He could have destroyed Pharaoh's army outright. Instead, He let the army corner the Israelites at a place where there is no escape. Then, when the end was apparently in site for this bedraggled band of refugees, God parted the Red Sea, orchestrated a miraculous escape, and destroyed the pursuing army. But why the last minute rescue? Perhaps it was to teach the Israelites not to rely on their own strength, but to fully depend on the Lord for deliverance. Unlike us, God is never worried about the timing. He knows exactly when action needs to be taken to address the challenges in our lives. Like the Israelites with their backs to the water, we need to learn to trust God, regardless of how distressing His timing seems to be. Can you obey His directive to the Israelite nation…"you need only to be still?"

Shadrach, Meshach and Abednego were righteous men of God, living in a foreign land after being taken there by the Babylonian army. Surrounded by unbelievers, they resisted the pressure to conform to the ways of the godless men and women around them. They were eventually forced to make a critical decision…to turn their backs on the one true God and live, or refuse to reject God and die. What did these three choose? They chose to continue worshiping the God who was their only hope. As a result, they were sentenced to death. These young seeming martyrs were put into a blazing furnace. To ensure their certain death, the king ordered that the fire be so hot that even the

Waiting on God

soldiers standing nearby were killed by the heat. Shadrach, Meshach and Abednego knew what was waiting for them and they knew it would be a horrible death. They trusted that God could rescue them, and I'm sure they prayed fervently for their deliverance. No help came. No cavalry to ride in and rescue them, no ruler to grant a pardon or stay of execution. When they were forced into the furnace, it must have seemed as final as it could possibly be. Suddenly in their midst, a fourth individual appeared, described by king Nebuchadnezzar as looking "like a son of the gods." (Daniel 3:25). Nebuchadnezzar ordered the men out of the furnace, and when these young men of God came out of the fire, everyone around them could see that "the fire had not harmed their bodies, nor was a hair of their heads singed; their robes were not scorched, and there was no smell of fire on them." (Daniel 3:27) Instead of a fiery death, deliverance had come. Rescue came at the last minute, but it came. The doubter among us might ask why God waited so long to save these men, who only wanted to be faithful to Him. Perhaps God wanted this miraculous intervention to serve as a testimony to those godless individuals around them. In fact, the Bible reports that king Nebuchadnezzar was so overwhelmed by what he had witnessed that he began worshiping the one true God. His powerful response was this…"Praise be to the God of Shadrach, Meshach and Abednego, who has sent His angel and rescued His servants! They trusted in Him, defied the king's command and were willing to give up their lives rather than serve or worship any god except their own God. Therefore I decree that the people of any nation or language who say anything against the God of Shadrach, Meshach and Abednego be cut into pieces and their houses turned into piles of rubble, for no other god can save in this way." (Daniel 3:28-29) What a dramatic change of heart that occurred in this unbelieving king, all because these three men were unwilling to abandon the hope that only the God of the universe could provide!

Like Shadrach, Meshach and Abednego, Daniel was a man who was completely devoted to the Lord. He too trusted God to rescue him from danger, even when rescue came at the last moment. He made a conscious decision to obey the Lord, even when he knew the dire consequences that awaited him because of that decision. Jealous administrators during the reign of King Darius sought to trap Daniel because of his integrity and trustworthiness. They convinced King Darius to issue an edict stating that anyone who worshipped any god or man other than the king would be thrown into the lion's den. They knew of Daniel's devotion to the Lord, and they were fairly certain that he wouldn't obey this edict. They were right. Daniel continued to pray three times a day and didn't try to hide his worship of the Lord. Bound by his own edict, King Darius was forced to issue a death sentence for his loyal servant. Daniel was thrown into the lion's den. At this point, would you think that there was any hope for him when he's surrounded by hungry lions? It certainly looked like the end of the road for poor Daniel. But once again

Waiting on God

God came to the rescue at the last minute. He sent an angel to shut the mouths of the lions, and Daniel's life was spared. Overjoyed that his friend had survived, and convinced that it was the hand of God that had rescued Daniel, King Darius issued a proclamation to everyone throughout the land. "I issue a decree that in every part of my kingdom people must fear and reverence the God of Daniel. For He is the living God and He endures forever; His kingdom will not be destroyed, His dominion will never end. He rescues and He saves, He performs signs and wonders in the heavens and on the earth. He has rescued Daniel from the power of the lions." (Daniel 6:26-27) Where there was no hope, God provided hope for a righteous individual that resulted in the conversion of an entire nation. And so it may be in your life. How might God use your response to a seemingly hopeless situation? Will you remain faithful until the very last hopeless moment? Will your steadfastness in a difficult situation serve as a bold witness to those who are begging for hope in their own lives?

Some years after Daniel's experience, another faithful servant of the Lord found himself in a seemingly hopeless situation. Mordecai was a Jewish exile who had been forced to leave his home when Nebuchadnezzar conquered Jerusalem. He and his cousin Esther lived under the reign of the Persian king Xerxes. Mordecai had adopted and cared for Esther after her parents had been killed. Through God's orchestrations, Esther was elevated in status to become Xerxe's queen. Because of

Mordecai's and Esther's actions, an assassination attempt on the king was thwarted. Despite their efforts on behalf of the king, they were despised by one of the king's nobles. Haman hated Mordecai because the latter would not honor him. By extension, Haman hated all the Jews and tricked king Xerxes into issuing an order that called for the extermination of all the Jewish people in the region. That included Mordecai and Esther. Haman was so sure his plan was bulletproof that he had a gallows built for Mordecai to be hanged on. It seemed that there was nothing that could be done to reverse the king's edict. Yet once again God was able to make a way out of desperate circumstances. Mordecai and Esther were able to turn the tables on Haman and expose his schemes. Once Xerxes realized the extent of Haman's scheming, he ordered Haman to be hanged on the very gallows that had been built for Mordecai! The king then issued another edict empowering the Jewish people to defend themselves against their enemies. Instead of the extermination of the Jewish people, their enemies met the fate intended for them. Although Mordecai, Esther and their fellow Jews surely sweated out the situation, God did not abandon them.

Peter, one of Jesus' disciples, must have had a feeling of what things were like when God took things down to the wire with him. The disciples were on King Herod's most wanted list after Christ's death and resurrection. Already, Herod had had James, the brother of John, put to death by the sword. When he realized how happy this made the Jewish ruling class, he had

Waiting on God

Peter arrested as well. A similar fate surely awaited Peter as it had for James. Unfortunately, there was no "get out of jail free card" for Peter. Or was there? We don't know how long Peter was in jail, but we do know that the night before his trial in Herod's kangaroo court, God sent an angel to help Peter escape. As bold a disciple as Peter was, he must have felt the proverbial noose tightening around his neck. Again, God could have intervened at any point prior to this, but he waited until the last minute.

How late would you think would be too late for God to intervene? Certainly, death would appear to be one of those conditions that most of us would consider permanent (strictly speaking in earthly, not spiritual terms now). If God hasn't healed a person before then, things certainly look pretty bleak, right? Well, not necessarily, especially where Jesus is concerned. Mary and Martha spent four agonizing days grieving over the death of their brother Lazarus. Although Jesus could have prevented Lazarus from dying, He didn't. In fact, when informed that Lazarus was sick, the Bible says that Jesus stayed where He was for two additional days. As a result, Lazarus died. For Lazarus' sisters, there appeared no hope for their brother now. This beloved brother of theirs was sick and dying, and Jesus, having a reputation for performing miracles, did nothing. Their prayers had fallen on apparently deaf ears. But we know from the Bible that this was not the end of the story. The waiting on the Lord that these sisters had done might have seemed futile,

The God of Hope

but Jesus knew better. The living Savior was not bound by the laws of biology. This God-made man, who would Himself be raised from the dead in order to save fallen man, knew that at God's command Lazarus would be returned whole to his sisters. Earthly death was no match for the true "resurrection and the life" found in Christ! No power, not even death, can separate us from our merciful Savior. After four days of facing death, Mary and Martha finally understood the unquenchable hope of everlasting life that comes from waiting on the Lord.

So what do *you* do when you have been holding on for so long, when you have fought the good fight of faith, but there still is no glimmer of hope on the horizon? You have bravely kept watch for even the slightest change in your circumstances, and listened intently for the smallest whisper from God, to no avail? You're at the point of physical, emotional and spiritual exhaustion, and just don't have the strength to keep going. What do you do? The answer is that you hang on. Now I don't mean to be trite or callous or coldhearted. Nothing could be farther from my intention. But having been at the bottom of the well, with not an ounce of water there to revive me, I have learned one of the hardest lessons of life. When you don't have the strength to take the next step and hope is nowhere to be seen, you hang on, for the alternative is not an option. When the rest of the world is telling you there is no point to hanging on, that it's a waste of time, that it's time to throw in the towel, you hang on. Don't listen to the world. When the devil tries to convince you that

Waiting on God

God has abandoned you, that God is looking unsympathetically down on your life in shambles, don't fall for his lies. Above all else you need to hold onto the truth - that God *is* there, and He *is* watching over you. He knows every detail of your situation, and nothing has happened in your life that has not passed through His hands first. However bad the situation looks, He has got it under control. Rest in the promise He made in the book of Isaiah, that "those who hope in the Lord will renew their strength. They will soar on wings like eagles; they will run and not grow weary, they will walk and not be faint." (Isaiah 40:31) At the moment of His choosing, God will send the rain clouds away and let the sun shine through. That's one thing that you must never doubt. Don't let the devil establish the beachhead that will lay the invasion route wide open for his victory. You're engaged in spiritual warfare, and the only way to gain the victory is to let the God of our only hope hold you in the palm of His hand and guide you safely down the path of His will.

I know the way is difficult. When we're exhausted, we're spiritually and emotionally vulnerable, and that's the time when the temptation to bypass God's hope is greatest. God knows how each of us is doing spiritually, but unfortunately the devil seems to be pretty good at knowing how we're doing too. You can be sure that Satan expends a great deal of energy trying to convince us that God cannot be relied upon, and that we must take action to save our own sinking ship. The hardest thing a person in despair often has to wrestle with is how long to wait on

The God of Hope

God before striking out in search of his/her own solution. Don't allow yourself to be tempted. Knowing the way the devil works is key to avoiding the traps he sets for us. When at your wit's end, make sure you seek God's face and not the devil's. God has promised that He will give you the strength to resist the devil. "But remember that the temptations that come into your life are no different from what others experience. And God is faithful. He will keep the temptation from becoming so strong that you can't stand up against it. When you are tempted, He will show you a way out so that you will not give in to it." (1 Corinthians 10:13, NLT) Are you willing to resist the temptation to do things your own way because you want to hurry things along? When you're tempted, remember all those who have gone before you, and be strengthened by their resolve. When Noah was in the ark for what seemed like forever, he held on. When Job suffered loss of family, possessions and health, he held on. When David faced danger daily while waiting to be king, he held on. When Joseph suffered injustice after injustice, he held on. All of these sojourners of faith, as humanly flawed as they were, chose to wait on God's hope rather than their own. Should we do any less than they?

Chapter 11

HELPING YOURSELF FIND HOPE

But in your hearts set apart Christ as Lord. Always be prepared to give an answer to everyone who asks you to give the reason for the hope that you have.
1 Peter 3: 15

Let us hold unswervingly to the hope we possess, for He who promised is faithful.
Hebrews 10: 24

The message emphasized throughout this book is one of turning to God for a hope that the world cannot provide. In reality, that can often be a difficult thing to do. Our natural tendencies of trying to maintain control and be self-sufficient often interfere with the process of letting God work His will in our lives. That being said, when we find ourselves waiting for God to answer our cries for help, what can we do while we're waiting? How can we be an active participant in this search for hope without circumventing the need to submit to God's will and timing?

The circumstances of life that lead us to the point of hopelessness drain us spiritually, physically, and emotionally. As a result, we end up neglecting ourselves in all three of those areas. Recognizing the ways in which hopelessness affects a person can go a long way in slowing the downward spiral, and might even help the person climb out of the pit that may seem inescapable. So let's focus on each one of these areas individually… the spiritual, physical, and emotional aspects of our lives. We'll start with what we can do to address the spiritual nature of hopelessness, for it represents the foundation which can then affect the physical and emotional aspects. If your spirit is currently crushed, where better to search for restoration than within the realm of the Almighty?

Like anything else in life, perfecting a skill or task requires effort, time and persistence. To strengthen your spiritual stamina, you must make that conscious effort to spend more time with God, who is the ultimate source of spiritual strength. Finding time in your schedule to engage God with your daily struggles may seem like a daunting task, but it's crucial to finding His hope. God already knows everything about you, but He wants you to know more and more about Him every day. How can you do this? The two best ways are also the most basic…reading His Word daily and opening up the line of communication with Him through prayer.

As much as your body needs food and water to survive, your spirit needs a daily dose of God's Word. There's nothing more essential to the strengthening of your soul than to arm yourself with the power of His divine Word. I challenge you to make a commitment to read the Bible every day. Not only will you come to know those heroes of faith who suffered the same trials and hopelessness that you may be facing today, but rest assured that the supernatural power of His Word will bring comfort to your soul in ways that you would never imagine. Immerse yourself in His Word and be amazed at the spiritual solace it can bring.

There are many different approaches to studying God's Word, but the most important thing is to open your Bible and start reading. Find a translation that works for you. If you're more old school, you might like the King James Version. If you appreciate a more modern translation, the New International Version might suit you better. There are even Bibles available which are specifically tailored to new believers. They contain background information and commentary that can be especially helpful to those just starting to learn about God. You can start at Genesis and read in historical fashion, or start at the beginning of the New Testament to focus more on Jesus Christ and the message of the Gospel. If you start diving into the Old Testament psalms, you'll find many of them were written by authors who were themselves weighed down by heavy burdens. They cried out to God for deliverance. Some of my favorites are Psalms thirty-seven, forty-six, seventy-three, and ninety-one. There are one hundred and fifty to choose from, and each one brings you in closer communion with the Father. For me personally, I start each morning with help from a daily devotional book that has a short message and Bible verses relevant to the day (usually Old/New Testament verses and a psalm). Then I read one chapter in Proverbs each day. Since there are thirty one chapters in Proverbs, it works out well for most months. After work, I try to read two or three chapters each day. Several years ago I decided to take on the challenge of reading the Bible from cover to cover. The first time through was certainly the hardest. Those chapters on the generations of descendants in the Old Testament were tough...I'll be the first to admit it. But God's presence becomes that much easier to sense the more you immerse yourself in His Word. It seems that each time I've read through the Bible in this way, God opens my eyes to new truths that He wants me to see. The inspiration for this book, Romans 15:13, was just another verse to me, until one day I read it again and saw it in a whole new light. Whatever time in the day that you can devote to studying His Word is definitely time well spent.

As important as daily Bible reading is to your spiritual health, so too is prayer. No more clear cut set of instructions for believers can be found than in 1 Thessalonians 5:16-17..."Be joyful always; pray continually." Other translations may state that as "pray without ceasing". Either way, the Bible makes it clear that prayer to God is something that we should always be doing. If life has you on the ropes right now, you may find it hard, if not impossible, to be joyful. When you're in the depths of depression, giving thanks for your current circumstances may be a little too hard to do. But prayer is something that's free,

Helping Yourself Find Hope

doesn't require any special equipment, and can be done at any time of the day or night. There's a handy little acronym that can help you in your prayer journey…A.C.T.S. This stands for adoration (A), confession (C), thanksgiving (T), and supplication (S). Notice that supplication, those things we ask God for, is at the end of the list. Most often we tend to hit God with our own concerns and needs first. That's part of the human equation, but we can all eventually learn to pray in a way that puts our priorities in the proper order. Don't beat yourself up if you don't feel you know the right way to pray. Like any physical exercise, the more we do it, the stronger our spiritual bodies become. As Martin Luther is credited with saying, "The fewer the words, the better the prayer"…and, "the less I pray, the harder it gets; the more I pray, the better it goes". A prayer lifted up to God in sincerity and humility is sweet music to His ears! You might even want to keep a prayer journal, where you can write down your prayer concerns and requests, and record how God has answered them. You may be amazed at how cathartic it is to write your feelings and thoughts down on paper. You may be even more amazed when you reread your journal and see how God has responded to your heartfelt prayers. If you're having trouble praying, allow the Holy Spirit to help you. That's one of His very important jobs…to act as intercessor for you and me when we cannot muster the right words to say in our daily talks with the Father.

The God of Hope

I know that the burdens and responsibilities of a person's life may make it seem like there isn't an extra moment in the day to read the Bible or pray. There's always one more thing that needs to be done, and twenty-four hours is just not enough time in each day to accomplish it all. But nothing is more important in the search for hope than to make this study of and dialogue with God a priority. The comfort and reassurance that comes from reading and digesting these divinely inspired words cannot be replaced by anything else. Neither can the power of prayer. Again, from the pen of Martin Luther, "Tomorrow I plan to work, work from early until late. In fact I have so much to do that I shall spend the first three hours in prayer". Three hours of daily prayer for the average working person is probably not an attainable goal. The point to be made is that starting your day with the Lord, and getting your will aligned with His early on, keeps your mind where it needs to be through whatever challenges the day may bring.

Do you remember that adopted cat of mine that you read about in chapter four? When this neighborhood stray first came to live with me, he was pretty happy with anything I fed him. Over time, though, he assumed the more typical feline attitude when it came to his food choices. He got as much dry food as he wanted throughout the day, but he knew at dinner time that he would usually get canned food or some other special treat. It didn't take him long at all to figure the system out, and his attitude then became not so much one of faint hope as one of vocal expectation. One day I was washing some dishes and he started to remind me that it was time for his treat. His internal clock rivaled the best timepieces money could buy. He started in his usual way of rubbing up against my legs and giving a few typical meows…the first clues he would throw out to let me know he was down there and hungry. I decided that I would finish with the dishes first, so I ignored the first volley of not so subtle hints. Well, he had learned that when you don't get what you want, you meow louder…and louder. I tried to ignore him, but he got so persistent and so loud that I finally gave in. Soapy hands and all, I made sure he got his treat. Often when he would carry on like that, I would be reminded of Luke eighteen and the parable of the persistent widow. In this parable, Jesus points out the need to persist in prayer even when it seems that no one is listening. How often do I say a prayer for something that is burdening my heart and yet end my prayers prematurely because I only halfheartedly believe that God will answer? Had that widow only persisted halfway, she would not have gotten the response from the judge that she did. I'm certainly not advocating becoming a nuisance to God or acting like a spoiled child who doesn't get their way. What I am suggesting is that we must firmly believe that God is listening and will answer our cries for help. Sometimes that may mean we need to be as relentless in prayer as that widow. I feel sheepish at times when I consider that my cat had more faith and hopeful expectation in my ability to respond to his needs than I have in God to provide for my own needs. In His silence, perhaps God is waiting to see how much we believe in His ability to provide, and how much faith and persistence we possess while we're waiting for an answer. The very words of Jesus support this. "Ask and it will be given to you; seek and you will find; knock and the door will be opened to you. For everyone who asks receives; he who seeks finds; and to him who knocks, the door will be opened. (Matthew 7:7-8) Like my cat, who had no problem getting his message across, we need to be so focused on our relationship with God that His ears never stop hearing our prayers! Just as my cat had his needs met, you can be assured that God will meet your needs as well. Not a bad lesson to learn from one very smart cat!

The spiritual challenges in your life may be compounded by the physical and emotional exhaustion often associated with hopelessness. When you're feeling the most hopeless, it usually means that the world has really worn you down. You try to make it through the day with your own strength, but you come to the realization that you just don't have any strength left. The thought of facing tomorrow, with all its new challenges, only exhausts you further. You can't remember the last time you met a new morning with enthusiasm. Think about it. We are an exhausted society, burning the candle at both ends and expecting that there won't be dire consequences because of it. When you're tired, you don't think as clearly as you should or focus on the healthy things in life. You don't have the gumption to maintain a positive attitude. When you're tired you often make the worst decisions when it comes to taking care of yourself. As important as anything, you need physical rest. Just as importantly, you need to give yourself permission to rest. God created each day with twenty four hours allocated to different activities. There's time to work, time to worship, time to eat, time to relax and time to sleep. Even God took a day off from creating the world we live in and He's God! He knows more about the needs of our bodies than oftentimes we do. Make sure that you allow yourself enough hours of sleep each night, and make sleep a daily priority. Too often we try to shortchange the rest our bodies need, and unknowingly lay the groundwork for exhaustion to creep into our lives. The world is moving at a faster and faster pace, and it's easy to get caught up in the cycle of trying to accomplish more things at the expense of our physical well-being. One of the great prophets of the Old Testament, Elijah, found this out the hard way.

Elijah had been engaged in a spiritual battle with Ahab, the wicked king of Israel. The last straw for Ahab was when Elijah had the prophets of the pagan god Baal killed. Ahab had reported the prophet's actions to his wife Jezebel, who then swore to kill Elijah in an act of revenge. Fearing for his life, Elijah fled. Exhausted, he sat down under a broom tree and prayed to God that he might die. "I have had enough, Lord…take my life; I am no better than my ancestors. Then he lay down under the tree and fell asleep" (1 Kings 19:4-5) How did God respond to Elijah's despair? He sent an angel to minister to this weary prophet. After Elijah had slept, the angel woke him up and brought him food to eat and water to drink. After Elijah ate and drank, he lay down again and rested some more. A second time the angel returned and brought more food and water for the prophet. Strengthened by these provisions, Elijah was then able to continue on with the Lord's work. If one of the greatest Biblical prophets needed to rest from his journey, how much more do we need to ensure that we rest, in order to have the strength to continue through the life that God has planned for us? Jesus' own words to His disciples should cement this need for rest in our daily lives. After the disciples had been so busy that they didn't even have time to eat, Jesus spoke these words to them, "Come with Me by yourselves to a quiet place and get some rest" (Mark 6:31)

As important as sleep is to refreshing your body, so too is exercise. For those who are physically limited and unable to exercise, I don't want to minimize the additional burden that this limitation imposes on you. Obviously, exercise is not a feasible option. For those who *are* physically able to exercise but are completely worn down, the last thing you want to do when you feel that way is exercise. You may be saying to yourself as you read this, "I don't even have the energy to get through the basic requirements of the day. How am I going to find the energy to exercise?" Or you might be thinking, "Why bother? It isn't like exercise is going to make any difference." In fact exercise, no matter how limited, does make a difference. Getting the heart pumping and getting moving can improve both your physical and mental state. You can try to trick your body into thinking that physical inactivity is okay, but God made us to be just the opposite. When you don't move, it compromises how efficiently you function. I'm not talking about signing up to run a triathlon or even running a half marathon. When a person is physically and emotionally exhausted, strenuous exercise may just add to their stress levels or emotional burden. But any exercise is better than none (of course check with your doctor before starting any exercise program). It may be just walking several blocks around your neighborhood or getting on a treadmill for 15 minutes. Start small. Getting outside on a sunny day can do a world of good in helping us see life in a more positive light. Go out and absorb some vitamin D! Instead of sending the family dog out into the backyard on his own, take him for a walk to the local park. It may well be just the boost your body and spirit need. There's no doubt that your dog will thank you for it…in his own four-footed way!

A nutritious diet is equally important in promoting a healthy physical lifestyle. Let me ask a question here…when you're physically and emotionally exhausted, do you tend to reach for the celery and carrot sticks, or do you head straight for the supersize bag of potato chips? For whatever reason, the unhealthy food choices are the ones that seem to be the easiest ones to make when we're down in the dumps. To me, macaroni and cheese is the quintessential comfort food. How about for you? I guess it's just part of human nature that we look for a ready source of comfort in what appears to be a comfortless world. Instead of turning to food for your comfort, would you be willing to turn to God for that comfort? I'll readily admit that it can be a difficult choice to make. The chocolate donut sitting on the kitchen counter is right there waiting for you. You can see it and feel it, while God can seem so far away. That donut is something you can hold in your hand, and each bite brings concrete, albeit short-lived, satisfaction. The only problem is that it's too soon gone, and so is the comfort that it brought you for those few short minutes. In fact, the only legacy it leaves is those pair of pants that don't quite fit as well as they used to. The temptation of comfort food does nothing to pull you out of that pit of despair. It may be stretching things to equate junk food with the devil. But I doubt that Satan would tempt anyone today with a piece of fruit, like he did Eve in the Garden of Eden. More than likely, his preferred weapon nowadays would be a thick slice of chocolate cake or a three cheese burrito.

When the canvas of your world is painted in dark colors, the last thing you want to do is take care of yourself. You feel as if eating for a healthy future is pointless because you can't see a future worth making the effort for. But God designed our bodies to reflect the best that He has to offer, and that includes the foods we put into our mouths. When you neglect to eat healthy foods, you're doing a disservice to the body that God has given you.

Helping Yourself Find Hope

There are enough scientific studies to confirm that our choice of foods affects not only our metabolism but our mood as well. While that junk food brings you momentary consolation, it takes its toll in other ways. The purpose of this book is certainly not to get heavy handed on nutrition principles or specific diet plans, but to emphasize that making even small changes toward a healthier diet can help in the battle against the unhealthy thinking that saps our spirit. Take those baby steps if need be. It may work better for you to change your diet one step at a time, rather than attempt a complete food makeover. And it might be good to remember a quote by Jack LaLanne, fitness expert of days gone by... "If man makes it, don't eat it!" If you have a choice between the short term satisfaction of potato chips and a soda, or the healthier benefit of a banana and water, try to make the tougher choice. It may take some getting used to, but if you can stick with healthier, it will eventually help lead your body to happier!

Acknowledging that physical lifestyle choices can impact your overall well-being is a solid place to start. So is acknowledging that your emotional well being affects how vulnerable you are to hopelessness. Positive changes in sleep, exercise and eating habits are great steps in the right direction. They don't address the emotional component of your situation, however. When you're feeling hopeless, there's a tendency to want to isolate yourself from the rest of the world. At such a low point, you feel the world has let you down. The last thing you want to do is involve yourself in anything that's likely to bring more stress and grief into your already overburdened life. As much as you may feel this way, you need to realize that further isolation increases those feelings of hopelessness. Have you ever heard the saying, "No man is an island?" It may seem contradictory, but in order to see God's glimmer of hope in this world, you need to engage this life, not withdraw from it.

One way to engage life is to find someone that you trust to talk with. Have someone in your life that you can unload your worries, concerns and anything else that you need to get off your chest. I realize that if you've been hurt by people in the past, this may not be an easy thing to do. But having even one or two persons in your life to whom you can unburden yourself, friends you can rely on, is a gift unlike few others in this world. Knowing that a friend has your back is a source of great earthly comfort. The book of Ecclesiastes says it very well: "Two are better than one, because they have a good return for their work: if one falls down, his friend can help him up. But pity the man who falls and has no one to help him up!"(Ecclesiastes 4:9-10). Jesus himself reiterates the importance of godly fellowship…"For where two or three are gathered together in My name, there am I in the midst of them." (Matthew 18:20, KJV) What a true comfort to know that God is at the heart of two friends united by His purpose!

While one or two friends can be of great comfort to a person in despair, the greater community of believers represents an army of support. If possible, try to find a local church that preaches the pure Gospel of Jesus Christ. Engage in the fellowship of many like-minded souls, people who are there to worship the one true God and support each other through good times and bad.

If you have a friend or two for support, or have a church to call home, that's great. But perhaps wounds caused by people have left you wary of human interaction. Maybe you're not quite ready to put yourself out there, only to be hurt again. That's completely understandable. If you feel that way, give yourself some time to get over the hurt. In the meantime, though, you might consider the companionship of a pet. Animals are sources of unconditional love, and the love that you can give them will by itself do much to cheer your soul. Countless studies have shown that having a pet to talk to and care for brings about positive changes in a person's life. Recent studies in medicine have shown that exercise can positively impact outcomes in cancer patients. To that end, there's a physician at Georgetown University who actually prescribes getting a dog for his patients, because he so believes in the benefits of walking them! So you see, pets like dogs can bring emotional <u>and</u> physical benefits…there's good reason they're called man's best friend! If you can't have a pet, consider volunteering at an animal shelter. The attention and love you provide these dogs and cats will be returned to you a hundredfold. Four-legged friends can be extremely good listeners, and I have never known an animal to judge. A purring kitten in your lap, or the expression of pure joy in a dog's face when they see you, is the most effective and cheapest form of medicine you can get!

In the course of trying to make it in this world, you can often settle into what is essentially survival mode. You focus on working to make ends meet, and how best to take care of your children, or elderly parents or anyone else that may depend on you (pets included, of course!). You wake up wondering how you're going to pay the bills, and how you're going to get everything done that needs to get done within the next twenty four hours. You don't have time to think about much else. You may be highly efficient, but after awhile that goal-oriented mentality takes its toll on you. You abandon things that you used to enjoy when you had free time. Even when you do get a few moments free, you would rather just vegetate than pick up an old hobby. Think back to when you were a kid, when you didn't have the weight of the world riding on your shoulders twenty-four seven. What things did you like to do? No matter how silly it may seem, find something that you used to enjoy, and do it. Did you love riding your bike as a kid, exploring every street as if it was a new frontier? Then get on your bike and rediscover that childlike joy that came when you pedaled just as fast as your little legs would take you, picking out an imaginary finish line in the distance and breaking the speed record for the mile! And in this instance, DON'T get on that bike because you need to burn some calories...do it because you just want to have fun with it.

Helping Yourself Find Hope

Did you enjoy going fishing? How about sewing or quilting or playing cards? Pick something that you can get excited about, something that's a healthy distraction from the burdens of the day. It doesn't need to be complicated or expensive. It just needs to be something that brings you a little joy in an otherwise stressful life. Give yourself half an hour to enjoy that every day. Make it a priority. You need that time to remind yourself that life can hold enjoyment for you once again.

Years ago when I was in college, a friend taught me how to cross-stitch. Cross-stitching is a form of embroidery that requires patience, focus and a bit of precision. A series of diagonal cross-shaped stitches are placed in a pattern that ultimately produces a design on the linen. For me, there is something very relaxing about laying down those stitches in sequence, and watching as the intended design takes shape. For years, though, I had put that hobby aside because there were just so many more important things to be spending my time on. Well, I was cleaning my house one day and came across a half finished project I had started several years earlier. I can't tell you how good it felt to take an hour out of the day to just relax and stitch on that linen. It may take me several more years to finish that project, but each time I allow myself to work on it, I reconnect with a balanced life…and it feels good.

I have a confession to make. When I was a kid, I loved to color. Back when I was growing up, I used to have those thick coloring books with a big old box of Crayola crayons. Not the overloaded activity books that kids have today, but just pages and pages of black and white outlines, waiting to be filled in with colors that were only limited by my imagination. As crazy as it may sound, one day I was thinking about coloring books and crayons and what fun I used to have. So during a visit to my local variety store, I picked up one of those vintage coloring books and a faithful box of sixty-four Crayola crayons, and I went to town. There's something about a fresh coloring book and a box of Crayolas that does a heart good! Coloring in the lines, while breathing in a whiff of that heavenly crayon scent, brought me back to a time when my biggest concern was when I could finish my homework so I could go outside and play. Please don't misunderstand me. I'm not advocating an escape from reality as an all consuming habit, but what I am trying to say is that it's okay to take a break from the adult sized burdens and responsibilities of your world for a little while. Sometimes silly is just what the doctor ordered. And now it seems that coloring books for adults are the latest trend…so maybe it's not so silly after all!

Another source of comfort and encouragement in my life is music. A great deal of satisfaction can be gained from the creating, playing or listening to of music. Since I'm musically challenged when it comes to playing an instrument (I seem to be the only one who can ever recognize the tune I'm playing), my greatest enjoyment is in the listening. I do a fair amount of driving in my profession, and having the radio on in the car helps me relax, or wax nostalgic depending on the song. It's amazing how one particular song from the 1980's can bring back a flood of great memories that instantly puts me in a better mood. In the area where I live, there are two stations that play contemporary Christian music all day long. Those stations take up the bulk of my listening time, and there always seems to be the right song playing to lift my spirit or encourage me whenever the inevitable challenges of the day hit. Never underestimate the power of music, or how God may use that music to minister to a hurting soul.

A striking example of the healing power of music involved a popular contemporary Christian song from the band "Third Day". Mac Powell, lead singer for the band, described the circumstances behind the band's song, "I Need a Miracle". At one performance, a couple came up after the show and described the impact that one of the band's songs had had on their son. It seemed that their son had been burdened by depression and addictions, and he was at a point where he was ready to take his own life. He drove out into the woods to end his life, but turned on the car radio and heard another of the band's songs, "Cry out to Jesus". The words of that song had such a profound impact on him, that he didn't take his life that day. In fact, his parents reported that at the time of the concert, their son was away on a mission trip. That's an amazing story of how God used one song at the perfect time in that man's life to bring him hope and renewed purpose. There's no limit to what God can or will use to open a person's heart to Him!

Whether it be through Bible study, prayer or even a song, the biggest challenge is learning to focus our thoughts on God, rather than ourselves and our problems. One of the most important things in laying the emotional groundwork for hope is to change the way we think. Of course, we all know that changing our thought process is much easier said than done. One of the hardest things to do when in the depths of despair is to change from a negative to positive attitude. We may even think that it's impossible, but recent research in the science of neuroplasticity has shown that we can actually change the way our brain functions by the way we think. I don't know why it's so much easier to focus on the negative in this life than on the positive. Someone once explained it to me this way. When we expect negative events, we're mentally preparing ourselves for when bad things eventually happen. In doing so, bad news doesn't come as a surprise, and the resulting pain or heartache isn't as great as it would be when we are taken off guard. When bad things happen in the face of an overly positive outlook, however, the impact it has on us is that much greater. From my own experiences, I suspect there is some truth to at least part of this explanation. I like to know what's coming down the road, and I habitually guard myself against catastrophe by expecting the worst. But since only God knows what the future holds for each of us, it's best not to dwell on all the unknowns of our tomorrows. Martin Luther had good advice when he said, "Pray, and let God worry". God has even better advice in the words of Matthew 6:34, "Therefore do not worry about tomorrow, for tomorrow will worry about itself. Each day has enough troubles of its own."

One of the critical factors in changing the way we think is to limit the question of "Why?" in life. When bad things happen or trials come, it's only natural to want to ask of God, "Why? Why is this happening to me? Why do I have to suffer like this? Why aren't you helping me God?" We want answers and we want to know there's a purpose for the suffering we're going through. The problem with asking too many whys, however, is that they do little to help us see the hope ahead of us, but instead foster doubt at the least and resentment towards God at the worst. The truth in life is that there is only one God and we're not Him. Only God knows fully how the pieces of our lives' puzzle fit together. He knows what's in store for us every single day of our lives, from birth to death, and the one thing he has promised comes from Jeremiah 29:11. "For I know the plans I have for you. Plans to help you and not harm you. Plans to give you hope and a future". Sometimes we just have to put aside the whys and instead lean on the God who can see the whole picture. Can you trust God through the many whys of your life? It's easier to do if you spend your energy listening to Him and not everything else in this world. Throughout your day, who are you most attentive to…God or the world around you? It's much easier to hear the shouting of the world telling you how bad things are. If you aren't hearing it from the TV or radio, I'm sure your relatives or next door neighbors have a story to tell about their misfortunes, health problems and the like. In fact, the roar of the world's problems can overshadow any message of hope that God is trying to send you if you're not making a conscious effort to hear Him. If need be, tune out the world for awhile. Limit your exposure to social media and other sources of bad news. Sometimes you just need a break from the constant news feed that serves to amplify uncertainties and anxieties, and leaves you wanting to shout at God, "Why"?

The prophet Elijah knew what it was like to hear the roar of the world, and it scared him. His life was dedicated to doing God's will, but his own people were trying to kill him because they didn't like the message that God had instructed him to tell them. Even after being attended to by an angel, and successfully escaping the evil intentions of Ahab and Jezebel, he was still despondent over the state of his life and the lives of the wayward Israelites. Elijah cried out to God, "I have been very zealous for the Lord God Almighty. The Israelites have rejected your covenant, broken down your altars, and put your prophets to death with the sword. I am the only one left, and now they are trying to kill me too." (1 Kings 19:10) What was God's reply to this beleaguered prophet? "The Lord said, 'Go out and stand on the mountain in the presence of the Lord, for the Lord is about to pass by.' Then a great and powerful wind tore the mountains

Helping Yourself Find Hope

apart and shattered the rocks before the Lord, but the Lord was not in the wind. After the wind there was an earthquake, but the Lord was not in the earthquake. After the earthquake came a fire, but the Lord was not in the fire. And after the fire came a gentle whisper. When Elijah heard it, he pulled his cloak over his face, and went out and stood at the mouth of the cave." As loud and frightening as the wind, earthquake, and fire must have been to Elijah, he strained his ears to hear God's gentle whisper. We, like Elijah, must learn to listen to the soft voice of our heavenly Father, rather than the noise of the world.

Who or what we decide to listen to is a choice, and it may well be one of the hardest choices you will have to make in your life. But the measure of true hope in your life ultimately depends on that choice. It's the difference between a life filled with the consolation of God's eternal promises and hopeful expectation of things to come, or a life weighed down by the burdens of the world and no earthly solutions offered.

The apostle Peter had a choice to make that day he and his fellow disciples were out on the Sea of Galilee. They had just witnessed the miracle of Jesus feeding the five thousand. He had instructed them to get into their boat and go on ahead of Him to the other side of the lake. Then during the night, the disciples suddenly see this figure coming to them, walking on the water. They had every reason to be terrified. Surely this must be a ghost, because no one can walk on water. Jesus says to them, "Take courage. It is I. Don't be afraid." (Matthew 14:27) Peter's response to Jesus is, "Lord, if it's You, tell me to come to You on the water." Notice Peter's hedge. Peter, the rock, prefaces his request with "if it's You". Regardless, Jesus tells him to come. Peter gets out of the boat and walks on water. He is defying the forces of gravity and doing the impossible. At that moment in time, he has made the right choice. He has crowded out any doubts with the reality of his Lord. He's doing what the world would say can't be done. Then, in a split second, the blink of an eye, something changes. Peter faces the wind and becomes afraid. At that moment he begins to sink, and cries out to Jesus, "Lord, save me!" How much like Peter are you and I? One minute we can maintain that focus on Jesus and tune the noise of the world out. Then all it takes is a split second to lose sight of our Savior, the One who can hold us up when we are sinking in the ocean of despair.

If you've ever heard Casting Crown's song "The Voice of Truth", you'll recognize the musical comparison to the predicament that Peter faced out on the water. The lyrics allude to the desire to have a faith that would enable the songwriter to step out onto the waves and reach for Jesus' hand. But remembrances of past failures and fear of the unknown cause great hesitation instead. It's only by listening to Christ's voice, the "Voice of Truth", that we can gain the strength to take that first important step of faith. The song ends with the wise admonition to listen to the "Voice of Truth" above all others.

Helping Yourself Find Hope

How can one weed out all the potential distractions that prevent us from keeping our eyes on Jesus? If you've ever been around carriage horses or race horses, you will sometimes see that the bridle of the horse is equipped with rectangular pieces of material that cover part of its' eyes. These are called blinkers, and they limit the horse's line of sight so that they can focus on what's ahead of them. These blinkers cut down on the things in the horse's peripheral vision that might distract it from its job. They can only look forward. They can't see anything to the side of them. As Christians, we need to equip ourselves with spiritual blinkers. We have to consciously focus on the hope that lies ahead of us, not all the distractions that would take our eyes off our Savior. All it takes is an instant to let the waves overtake us. It's a choice, and however difficult it may be, our efforts should be spent concentrating on the One to whom true hope belongs.

The more you can center your life around the blessings that God has provided for you and your loved ones, the firmer your footing on the path to hope will be. Although it may be difficult to see any blessings in your daily life right now, the key is to start small and think of one or two things that spark the tiniest flicker of hope. Whatever the challenges of the day, if you're reading this book right now, it means that God has given you life, the most precious gift of all. It means that God has given you eyes that can see and a mind that can understand. If you're blessed with a job, what do you see on the way to work? In spring, do you see the budding trees and the beautiful tapestry of purples and yellows as the crocuses and daffodils break free of their winter prison? How about a friend or loved one who calls you out of the blue just to say hello and let you know that they were thinking about you? There are things all around that remind us of God's love for us. The trick is to not let the world crowd them out of our vision. Develop practices in your life that encourage hopefulness and foster a thankful spirit. Plant a garden or start a project that reflects hope for the future. Nothing supports a hopeful attitude more than to emerge from the cold bleakness of winter and be witness to the first emerging spring flowers and new leaves on the trees. The renewal of life gives us all a lot to be thankful for. If you can follow the advice of a popular saying, "Count your days in smiles not tears, count your age in blessings, not years", then you are on your way to a more properly focused life.

By fostering an attitude of thankfulness, you make an all important acknowledgement to the Lord that you appreciate the blessings He has given you. Oftentimes when faced with the challenges of life and the expectation that nothing about our situation will improve, it's difficult to be thankful for even the little things. It's equally important that we make a conscious effort to give thanks for the good we do experience in our daily lives. While your circumstances may seem grim, it's essential that you not allow life's hardships to overshadow the things you have to be thankful for. Consider the case of Jesus and the ten lepers. In Jesus' travels, he came upon ten men who had leprosy.

Helping Yourself Find Hope

They were social outcasts and had to be feeling that their situation was hopeless. Leprosy was an incurable disease. When they saw Jesus they cried out to Him "Have pity on us!" Jesus instructed them to go and show themselves to the priests, and while on their way they were healed. Although ten were healed, only one man out of the group, a Samaritan, returned to thank Jesus for what He had done. Jesus asked the man, "Were not all ten cleansed? Where are the other nine? Was no one found to return and give praise to God except this foreigner? (Luke 17:17-18) My question to you is this…who would you rather be like - that one Samaritan who was truly thankful, or the other nine men who hadn't the time or inclination to thank Jesus?

A 2003 paper by psychologists Robert Emmons and Michael McCullough focused on the potential benefits of a grateful attitude in one's life. They conducted three studies which looked at the effects of gratitude on the participants' sense of well-being. The combined findings of these studies suggested that those individuals who maintained a grateful outlook felt better about life, were more optimistic about the future, had fewer physical complaints, slept better and exercised more. In addition, those grateful individuals were then more likely to help others and provide support to them. All that came from simply fostering an attitude of thankfulness. But is that really a surprise? Could it be that God had that in mind when He issued His directive to "give thanks in all circumstances, for this is God's will for you in Christ Jesus"? (1 Thessalonians 5:18)

The God of Hope

When you're on the receiving end of someone's kindness, it can give you a lot to be thankful for. But have you ever considered that being the one who performs an act of kindness can bring about its own profound change in your attitude? Whoever is credited with the adage "it's better to give than to receive" must have benefited from the wisdom of those words. There's something very satisfying in spending time outside ourselves, in focusing on the needs and concerns of others. The consolation that you might be able to provide them in their time of despair can be immeasurable. You may be *the* one to make all the difference in their lives.

I have a plaque hanging on the wall of my living room. It's a great reminder to me of what one person can do to make the world a better place. This is what it says:

If you planted hope today, in any hopeless heart
If someone's burden was lighter because you did your part
If you caused a laugh that chased a tear away
If tonight your name is mentioned when someone kneels to pray
Then your day was well spent.

They're simple words, but consider their impact. Is there something that you can do today for a friend or loved one, to ease their particular burdens? It doesn't have to be something major, just something to let them know that they matter and they haven't been forgotten. Then see how that one small act of kindness can snowball into positive results for them and you. There are countless "small things" that can be done for a relative, friend or neighbor. Checking up on an elderly widow in your neighborhood may not seem like a big deal, but to that woman you may be the only person reflecting Christ's love to her for the entire week. There are so many worthwhile organizations dedicated to helping individuals and families...the Salvation Army, Samaritan's Purse, Habitat for Humanity are just a few. If you don't have the funds to donate to these charities, perhaps you can donate your time. Maybe you can partner with your local community of believers and help within your own neighborhood. Many churches have food pantries and homeless ministries to help those who need assistance. Even if you can't physically help, you can still do one of the most important things - pray! Never underestimate the power of your petitions to God on behalf of someone else. There are even online ministries where you can volunteer to share the Gospel and pray for the needs of others. The opportunities are all around us. We just need to pick one and run with it!

In the end, it's the combined health of our spirit, mind and body that help us weather the storms of life. While we're waiting on God for answers, the suggestions in this chapter are designed to help us maintain the godly, rather than earthly, perspective in our lives. We must always remember, however, that our lives are not on our own timetable, but rather on God's. We must resist the strong urge to take the reins and try to control

The God of Hope

our own destiny in this search for hope. In this regard, I especially like a nineteenth century quote. This verse speaks of happiness, but I think it applies equally well to our search for hope. "Happiness is like a butterfly, which when pursued, is always beyond our grasp, but which, if you will sit down quietly, may alight upon you". The harder we try to find our own hope, the more elusive it is. The toughest thing to do is to actively let go and allow yourself to be held by God. Don't try to have all the answers to life's questions…it's impossible. When we loosen our grip and let God take us by the hand, He'll be able to provide that permanent hope which does not disappoint.

Chapter 12

JESUS, THE ULTIMATE SOURCE OF HOPE

And so, Lord, where do I put my hope? My only hope is in You.
Psalm 39:7 NLT

Blessed is the man who perseveres under trial, because when he has stood the test, he will receive the crown of life that God has promised to those who love Him.
James 1: 12

    I'm sure by this point you don't need me to tell you that life is hard. Because of original sin, the life that God intended for us is no longer possible. The perfect world that God created has been replaced by one where sin exacts a harsh toll on every person. None of us can escape the consequence of what Adam and Eve did in the Garden of Eden. While we may think it's unfair to have to bear the responsibility of someone else's sin, that's just the reality of life. The question is, given the hardship that original sin has created in life, how will you respond to those things in your life that want to steal all sense of hope from you? Will you let those difficult circumstances drive a wedge between you and God, or will you allow God to use life's hardships to guide you to a place where He wants you to be?

The God of Hope

It can be difficult to reconcile that the same God who has allowed you to experience the difficulties you are facing is the same God who wants to provide you with His hope. It's the age old irony of good things resulting from bad circumstances. Yet human nature being what it is, would we really be able to find hope any other way? If life were perfect and we faced no hardship, would we be as willing to turn to the one true God as when everything is falling down around us? For those of us who can recall the tragic events and horrible loss surrounding 9/11, can you remember the response of the country in the weeks after the terrorist attacks? Houses of worship were filled to capacity with individuals trying to make sense out of what had happened. People were searching for some measure of comfort and solace because the very foundation of their lives had been so badly shaken. So many of us want to shut God out of the picture as we vainly attempt to control our own destiny. Often it is only through the difficulties in life that it seems God is able to get our attention. Have you ever considered that God's love for us is so great that He doesn't want us to search for or accept any other hope but His own? He knows that what He offers is a deep and abiding hope that will never disappoint. While it's true that God is the provider of that ultimate hope, each of us has to be willing to accept it. I know that I often have a hard time admitting this. How about you? I really do want to accept that things can be as simple as acknowledging God and taking Him at His word, but for some reason I have trouble doing it. Why is it so hard to believe that things could be that simple? When God says that He has everything under control, that the very hairs of our head are numbered and that not one sparrow falls to the ground without His knowing about it, I desperately want to believe Him…but in reality I struggle. It's the daily battle between the seen and the unseen, the problems I face versus the promises of God, faith versus doubt. It's easy to stew over the "what ifs" that distract us from focusing on the ultimate goal. Can you really believe what God has promised? I'm pretty good at hearing the world's declarations of doubt but oftentimes am stone deaf when God is speaking. It ultimately comes down to a choice. Do we take God at face value and believe what He tells us in His Word, or do we choose to doubt Him? The following verse does a good job of describing this choice to be made:

> It takes a lot of courage to put things in God's hands,
> To give ourselves completely, our lives, our hopes, our plans
> To follow where He leads us, and make His will our own
> But all it takes is foolishness to go the way alone

Are you walking the road to hope on your own, or are you ready for someone to walk beside you?

The movie, "The Shawshank Redemption", explores the significance of hope between two friends in a decidedly secular way. Its' overwhelming theme of hopefulness despite life's hardships serves to underscore the absolute necessity of hope for

The God of Hope

the human condition. Andy Dufresne, the main character, has been imprisoned for allegedly murdering his wife. He really is innocent, but still ends up convicted of the crime. Sent to prison, he is abused by his fellow inmates, brutally beaten by the prison guards, and exploited for financial gain by the prison warden. His existence is a life gone very wrong for a man innocent of any crime. Despite all of his mistreatment, Andy maintains hope that one day he will be exonerated. He makes friends with Red, a longtime inmate and now very cynical fellow, who marvels at Andy's ability to maintain hopefulness in the midst of this harsh prison life. Red sees hope as an object to be despised because it denies what he thinks is life's reality. One day, a new prisoner arrives who has proof that Andy is indeed innocent. Finally, Andy realizes that this is his chance at freedom. But the corrupt prison warden is worried that this new prisoner will derail his plans of using Andy to embezzle prison funds. The warden arranges to have the new prisoner murdered in what is reported as an escape attempt. At first Andy is inconsolable at the death of the one man who could have proven his innocence. Red wonders if his friend has finally hit rock bottom, and worries that Andy may have now given up on life. It's an especially dark period for the both of them. Somehow, through it all, Andy still has a glimmer of hope flickering deep in his soul. In his mind, he can envision a secret and solitary place of hope and peace, the place he's planning to escape to. The walls and bars of the prison are of little consequence to Andy. He has calculated his path to freedom with excruciating detail. Red thinks that his friend has surely lost all touch with reality, as a prison escape appears impossible. But Andy has that unwavering focus, and allows himself no distractions in achieving this singular purpose. One dark night, in the middle of a deafening thunderstorm, Andy breaks free of that prison and begins his journey to the small town he has been dreaming of. The hope he held onto in that prison for so many years has finally been realized. The movie could have ended there and viewers might have been satisfied. Andy, however, has not forgotten his friend back in prison. Red, the cynic who has no use for hope, cannot help but be affected by his friend's unwavering measure of the same. One day he receives an anonymous postcard with cryptic instructions for when he is released from prison. Finally the day of his release comes. Now Red has a choice to make. Does he accept life as he is used to seeing it and try to survive in a world currently unfamiliar to him, or does he dare grab hold of the hope that his friend Andy embraced? In a nod to this power of hopefulness, the final scene of the movie depicts Red and his friend reuniting in the place that had once seemed an impossibility for them both. In the end, it is his friend's unwavering conviction that shows Red the light and teaches him that hope can bring you through the most difficult of circumstances to a new life. Although a secular movie, it serves as a nice parallel to our spiritual journey. As in life, there is one of two ways to travel…with or without hope. When there is no hope, the journey is a long and painful one, and maybe there is a point where we're not willing to move along any further down the road. With hope, no matter how difficult the circumstances, we are equipped to handle whatever life throws at us so that we can make it successfully to our eternal home. Our only real source of hope comes from the One who supplies everything else we need for the journey. Life represents a very hollow existence without that assurance of a future hope.

The "Shawshank Redemption" may be a work of fiction, but it does a good job of addressing the difficulties of maintaining hope in a seemingly hopeless situation. Personality differences may leave us more or less vulnerable to the effects of hopelessness, and certainly friends may lessen the burdens we bear through life's journey. Inevitably our human frailties can leave us vulnerable to eventual despair, where our best attempts to repel the effects of life's painful experiences begin to fail. Where then does our stamina to continue the fight come from? As in this movie, the trials we face in this life are made more bearable when we have someone walking beside us. The reality is that our quest for hope should not be a solo expedition. We were never meant to tackle the problems of life head on and without help. God is the true source of hope that will sustain us throughout the trials and sorrow of this life. Yes, the heartaches and pain will come. While God may protect us from certain hardships, we are certain to be affected by other suffering. That's why it is all the more important to embrace those words of

Jesus the Ultimate Source of Hope

Roman 15:13. Let God fill you with His hope, and let the power of the Holy Spirit intercede on your behalf. Your responsibility is simply to allow God to walk beside you and fill you with the hope that comes from the sacrifice that His Son made for all of us. The more active a role you allow God to take in your life, the more joy and peace you will experience. There is no self-serve when it comes to hope. All man-made avenues to hope lead to dead ends and a void we are unable to fill without Him. Just think about it. No matter what you're going through right now or what you may face in the future, it pales in comparison to what is waiting for you at the end of your life's journey. However great the pain you have experienced throughout your life, there will be a day when there will be no more pain, no more tears, and no more grief. Can you imagine that day when there will be no more suffering - nothing but joy, contentment and peace? You'll never know worry or fear again. Illness, loss and heartache will be non-existent and the joy and peace that we'll experience will last forever. Isn't that a hope that you want for your life? It's a hope that is found only at the foot of the cross of our resurrected Savior.

True hope doesn't lie in the solutions that the world has to offer. Contrary to what we may have been led to believe, hope doesn't come from a fat bank account or material wealth. How many times have you read or heard about wealthy businessmen who had the fancy house and cars, the speedboats and private jets, and yet were miserable because their lives were in shambles. With that amount of material abundance, they should be overflowing with hope, but it just doesn't seem to play out that way. True hope doesn't come from political promises or government assurances, from fame, or any other success that the world has to offer. Those things are temporary, and in large part rely on the shaky foundations and inherent untrustworthiness of the human condition. There's only one true source of hope in this life, and He died on the cross over two thousand years ago to give us, even we who were not yet born, the truest hope that will sustain us through whatever this life will subject us to. Because Christ lives, we can face an unknown number of tomorrows, despite whatever pain or good they may bring.

In a sense, I think most of us are searching for a "happily ever after" life here on earth. You know the kind…one that might have some suffering for awhile, but ends up with all trials and conflicts neatly resolved after a time and then nothing but a happy future. It's a lot like those movies or television shows, where there's high drama for an hour or two but by the end every problem has been solved. As a child I remember going to the movies and seeing a film titled "Seven Alone". It was a fictionalized depiction of a real life family traveling the Oregon Trail during the mid 1800's. I didn't remember too much about the movie other than the seven alone referred to the seven children who had to travel the trail by themselves after their parents had died. I had pretty much forgotten the movie even existed until I happened to catch it on television one evening.

Jesus the Ultimate Source of Hope

True to form, these seven orphans braved terrible hardship but ultimately all survived the journey. At the end of the movie, they arrive at a local mission and are adopted by a caring couple. That seems like a happy ending, right? I became a little curious about the real life Sager family portrayed in the film, and started searching for more information on the pioneer orphans. What I discovered was that the happy ending that the movie depicted wasn't so happy after all. Catherine Sager Pringle, one of the children, wrote a journal of her family's travels. It seemed her father was a restless soul, who had the family moving often, always in search of something better. Here was a man who seemingly did not have a sense of peace and was trying to find something to give him that peace. Uprooting his family from a more settled life, they join one of the early wagon trains traveling to Oregon. While on the trail, both father and mother succumb to illness, leaving the seven children ranging in age from fourteen years to newborn infant, amongst the other pioneer families in the wagon train. When they finally reached the West Coast, the children were in fact adopted by the Whitmans, a kind missionary couple. But a short three years after their adoption, an Indian attack on the mission left both the Whitmans and the two oldest children dead, and the remaining girls held captive by the Indians. Three of the four girls survived this unspeakable ordeal, but it's likely the trauma of what they witnessed stayed with them for the rest of their lives. The youngest child, Henrietta, later died at the age of twenty-six after being shot by an outlaw.

The God of Hope

While this family's story is a tragic one, there were and are countless other families who suffered as much if not worse hardships. For them, "happily ever after" was nothing more than a faraway dream. The tragic events of one's life serve to underscore that hope in an earthly life can often lead to much disappointment and despair. Does that mean that God has forgotten us or that He enjoys seeing us suffer? Not at all! All the suffering should serve as a reminder that earth is not our permanent home. We long for the consolation of our eternal home, with the peace and love that only our heavenly Father can provide.

One thing you must engrave upon your heart. Always remember that you are precious in God's eyes! You are His unique creation…there is no one just like you and you are of infinite worth to Him. That may be hard to accept when you are in the midst of great pain. It may be hard to hear when the world is trying to tell you that God doesn't care about you. Don't listen to the world's lies, though. I don't know why we choose to doubt God's love for us, while at the same time embracing the world's disdain for us. But the fact is we do. What you must always remember is that God had a plan for you well before you were born and He has a definite purpose for your life right now. In order to fulfill His purpose for you, you have to recapture that energy that life has drained from you. In order to do that, you have to take care of yourself in the same way that God wants to take care of you. That's why as people of faith, we must learn

Jesus the Ultimate Source of Hope

not to focus on the future through the eyes of the world, which so often are clouded by the cataracts of this earthly life. Instead, we must focus on the future that has been secured for us by the sacrifice of our Lord and Savior Jesus Christ. No matter how bad things get for you in this life, belief in the crucifixion and resurrection of Jesus Christ guarantees you an eternal life that knows none of the pain and suffering that you have experienced here on earth. I wish I could say to you that everything from this point forward is going to be a "happily ever after life" if only you place your trust in Jesus. Unfortunately that will probably not be the case. We live in a fallen world and bad things happen all the time. Believing in Christ does not ensure that you will never lose your job or your home, that your children will never see heartache or tragedy, or that you won't live out your life in loneliness and isolation. There are plenty of Christians who are good people, and who strive to follow God's will for their lives and yet still suffer illness and financial hardship. The hope for us comes from the knowledge that these things, as hard as they are to live with during our earthly tenure, are only temporary. Whether God provides relief for your particular situation while here on earth or not, you have the assurance that once you enter into His eternal presence, your perfect life begins.

When I was in college, my mother gave me a little stone plaque that now sits on the desk where I conduct my daily Bible study. The plaque reads, "Because He lives I can face tomorrow". At the time I was grateful for my mother's gift and

The God of Hope

her thoughtfulness, but the words of that plaque didn't make the impression on me that they should have. You see, I didn't fully understand the real significance of those words because I hadn't yet faced the trials and hardships that would bring clarity to them. In the years since I first received that plaque, each new challenge in life has sharpened my focus and comprehension of those words. Now I understand how those words can bring strength to a day filled with trouble and anxiety. Now I finally understand why those words can bring a comfort greater than any comfort the world can provide. When I cannot by my own strength make it through another day, when I look to the future and all I see is more suffering in the world and more bad news and despair, I think of those words and the solace they bring. Because Jesus came to this earth and lived the life He lived, because He allowed Himself to be crucified on a cross and bear the sins of the entire world, because He has given salvation through faith in His death and resurrection, I can face tomorrow with confidence because I know where I will eventually end up…in His loving arms. No matter how bad life gets, and no matter how long those bad times may last, I know that when my life on this earth ends, as it will for everyone, I will run into the loving embrace of my Savior and finally realize that everlasting hope for which my soul has been yearning since the day of my birth. That's the true hope to which we cling, a hope that cannot be extinguished no matter what earthly circumstances exist in our lives.

Jesus the Ultimate Source of Hope

In the classic hymn, "My Hope is built on Nothing Less", author Edward Mote addresses this everlasting truth:

> My hope is built on nothing less
> Than Jesus' blood and righteousness;
> I dare not trust the sweetest frame,
> But wholly lean on Jesus' name.
> On Christ, the solid Rock, I stand;
> All other ground is sinking sand.
>
> When darkness veils His lovely face,
> I rest on His unchanging grace;
> In every high and stormy gale
> My anchor holds within the veil.
> On Christ, the solid Rock, I stand;
> All other ground is sinking sand.
>
> His oath, His covenant, and blood
> Support me in the whelming flood;
> When every earthly prop gives way,
> He then is all my Hope and Stay.
> On Christ, the solid Rock, I stand;
> All other ground is sinking sand.
>
> When He shall come with trumpet sound,
> Oh, may I then in Him be found,
> Clothed in His righteousness alone,

The God of Hope

> Faultless to stand before the throne!
> On Christ, the solid Rock, I stand;
> All other ground is sinking sand.

Are you willing to make Christ your solid rock in the midst of every storm that might come into your life?

If you choose to take God at His word, then you need to know that the devil is going to engage you in a battle of the mind. His tactics are going to be relentless and underhanded as he works tirelessly to get you to throw in the towel. You can't allow him to gain a toehold in the door, or before you realize it that door will be flung wide open and what hope you have will be snatched from you. Don't allow yourself the luxury of even one "what if". One "what if" can snowball into full fledged doubt. None of us is bulletproof when it comes to Satan's attacks. The chinks in our armor, self-centeredness and pride, can leave us mortally wounded on the spiritual battlefield. Pride doesn't like admitting that we aren't in control of our lives…it doesn't like facing the fact that God is ultimately in charge. When we wrestle control away from God, we then have to assume the burdens and responsibilities that come along with the job. I don't know too many people who can successfully bear the full weight of the world's burdens without help from God. Do you?

If relinquishing control of your life to God still seems too hard to do, then look back to the examples of God's faithful people that have been previously discussed. The many heroes of

Jesus the Ultimate Source of Hope

the Bible fought the good fight of faith to grab hold of the hope that God had promised them. Elijah and Elisha, Joshua and Caleb, Gideon and his small army all faced situations that seemed hopeless when considering their own strength. In all these instances, the individuals looked at the future with a certain sense of fear and doubt. Yet they clung to the promises that their heavenly Father had given them. They relied upon the Lord for their deliverance, and He didn't disappoint them. His sovereignty ruled the day. Fixing our eyes on the author and perfecter of our faith makes all the difference in how we hold on through the tough times.

Simeon was a man described in the Bible as righteous and devout. He was in Jerusalem when Joseph and Mary had brought the young Jesus to the city in order to present Him to the Lord. Simeon had been told by the Holy Spirit that he wouldn't die before he had seen the Christ child. Can you imagine what Simeon must have been thinking about while he waited for his Savior? All his hopes for himself and Israel were tied up in the destiny of this young child. Here he would have the opportunity to see the Son of God in the flesh. When he went to the temple courts and finally laid eyes on the Savior of the world, I imagine he must have been overwhelmed with joy at the prospect of looking into the face of his living Savior. He took Jesus in his arms and praised God, saying, "Sovereign Lord, as you have promised, you now dismiss your servant in peace. For my eyes have seen your salvation, which you have prepared in the sight of all people, a light for revelation to the Gentiles and for glory to your people Israel" (Luke 2:29-32). This song of Simeon, as it's often called, is the basis for the Nunc Dimittis (Latin for "now you dismiss"), the closing portion of many church services even today. Simeon's words speak to that hope upon which all salvation is based. His patient endurance was rewarded when he was able to hold his Savior in his arms. Any previous suffering and tragedy in this man's life was forgotten when he came face to face with the embodiment of the living Hope that is Jesus Christ.

Stephen, one of the early disciples who preached and performed miraculous signs among the Jews, was a man full of God's grace and power. His faith in the hope of the Savior drew opposition from the Jewish Sanhedrin. Because of his outspoken preaching and devotion to his risen Lord, he was a threat to the Jewish status quo. Stephen knew full well where the only hope for himself and the Jewish people lay. In the midst of a threatening crowd, yet full of the Holy Spirit, he looked up to heaven and saw the glory of God, and Jesus standing at the right hand of His Father. "Look", he told the crowd, "I see heaven open and the Son of God standing at the right hand of God." (Acts 7:56) Stephen's eyes had been opened to the truth of salvation while those around him remained blinded to that same truth. They could not or would not embrace Jesus Christ as the only way to salvation. In their rage, they stoned Stephen to death, and he became one of the first martyrs of the Christian faith. But death for Stephen was merely the fulfillment of Christ's resurrection hope. While he faced earthly death, Stephen understood that the end of his life on earth meant the beginning of his eternal life with Christ.

Mary Magdalene, another follower of Jesus, knew what it meant to live without hope. From the Bible we know that at one time she had been possessed by not one, but seven demons. How her life must have changed when Jesus drove those demons out of her. She may not have known much about this Jesus at first: that He was to be the fulfillment of Old Testament prophecy, but she bore witness to the fact that He was someone very different. As she spent more time with Him, it might have been easier to believe that He was in fact the Savior of the world. Certainly no one else could do the things He did or teach the people as He did. Her belief gradually strengthened. Yet when Jesus was crucified, it seemed that her hope was misplaced. After all, most of the disciples and other followers seemed to accept their Lord's death as final. Despite what Jesus had told them, their doubts had gotten the better of them. Imagine the range of emotions Mary must have experienced when at the tomb on that first Easter morning. Grief was surely the order of the day, then confusion and terror when she saw the stone rolled away from the tomb and the angel of the Lord present where Jesus had been. Finally, when Jesus Himself stood in front of her, it must have then become clear that all the hope she had put in Him was not misplaced after all. He was who He said He was and her world would never be the same. She too had met the Living Hope!

Simeon, Stephen and Mary Magdalene were just a few of those individuals who looked to Jesus Christ as the ultimate fulfillment of their hope. While it's true that we don't have the advantage of holding the Christ child in our arms as Simeon did, or witnessing Christ's resurrection as Mary did, we have the life changing experiences of those followers who came before. We have the Word of God and we have the Holy Spirit. Steven, that early Christian martyr, was full of the Holy Spirit, when during the last moments of his life he was able to look to heaven and see Jesus standing at God's right hand. All his sacrifices and all the anguish associated with a life dedicated to following God's will, were rewarded by that vision of Christ. His suffering faded as the light of Christ outshone all the pain. So it can be for us. We can stand on the promises in the Word of God and rest on the assurance that those promises are true.

God never meant for us to face the challenges of this life alone. As isolated and alone as we may feel, God's presence is real and immutable. He has provided us with the Holy Spirit, our intercessor, who guides us in our daily struggles. The words of Romans 8:26 reassure us of this…"In the same way, the Spirit helps us in our weakness. We do not know what we ought to pray for, but the Spirit Himself intercedes for us with groans that words cannot express". How comforting is that knowledge to you? Have you ever been in such a painful place that you didn't even know how to talk with God? Have you ever been so exhausted that you couldn't even muster the right words to ask for help? Well, God knows. I particularly love that phrase "with groans that words cannot express". I have been there, overwhelmed by a mix of raw emotions…pain, uncertainty, frustration, all rolled up into one big heap of helplessness that can't be articulated with anything more than groans. But it's okay. God hears and He understands. If you're empty, God wants to fill you up with His joy and His peace. Not the peace that the world gives, but a true and lasting peace. But you have to believe in Him and His ability to do it. It's one of the hardest choices that you may make in your life, but it's certainly the most important. Let the Holy Spirit come into your heart and not just fill it, but *overflow* it with the one true hope that overcomes anything you may face in this world…the hope of Jesus Christ and eternal life with Him.

We can try to convince ourselves that we can't measure up to the Biblical heroes of the Old Testament. We don't have their strength or their determination. That may be true. You may be so exhausted that you can't see how on earth you're going to hold on for another day. But what we do have in common with these individuals is that we are children of God. On our own, we may not have what we need to fight the good fight of faith, but with Almighty God holding us up, we have every reason to be hopeful for tomorrow. The devil is no match for our living God. One day the Lord will completely and utterly vanquish Satan, the destroyer of hope. Then we will spend eternity with the author and supplier of all hope, Jesus Christ. One day the deepest yearnings of our hearts will be fulfilled and the momentary struggles of this life will be replaced by the abundance of God's grace. Take heart, my friend, because there is a joyous hope waiting for you in the person of Jesus Christ. He is the one who will never disappoint in this life or the life eternal. Let Jesus be your never-ending source of true Hope!

SOURCES

Chapter 2

"TheRedSeaCrossing."ArkDiscovery.http://www.arkdiscovery.com/red_sea_crossing.htm

Casting Crowns. The Voice of Truth. *Casting Crowns.* Beach Street Records, 2003

Associated Press. "Ethiopian Girl Reportedly Guarded by Lions." Posted June 21, 2005. MSNBC.com. www.nbcnews.com/id/8305836/?GT1=1&displaymode=1098. Accessed June 22, 2005.

Associated Press. "Pregnant Skydiver Survives Parachute Malfunction." Posted December 13, 2005. Fox News. www.foxnews.com/story/2005/12/13/pregnant-skydiver-survives-parachute-malfunction.html. Accessed March 19, 2013

Chapter 3

Luther, Martin. The Lord's Prayer. Luther's Small Catechism. CPH.org. www.catechism.cph.org/en/lords-prayer.html.

Chapter 4

ABC News. "Medical Miracle: Woman Back from Brink of Death". Posted February 14, 2008. ABC News. www.abcnews.go.com/GMA/OnCall/story?id=4290829

Brantly, Dr. Kent. "Dr. Kent Brantly: I am Thrilled to be Alive". Posted July 20, 2015. Billy Graham Evangelistic Association. www://billygraham.org/story/dr-kent-brantly-prepared-remarks-i-am-thrilled-to-be-alive/

Goodman, Brenda. "The Race to save Dr. Brantly: The Inside Story". Posted September 12, 2014. Webmd. www.webmd.com/news/20140912/saving-kent-brantly

ABC News. "Randy Pausch, 'Last Lecture' Professor Dies. Posted July 25,2008. https://abcnews.go.com/GMA/randy-pausch-lecture-professor-dies/story?id=4614281. Accessed May 20, 2018

Joni Eareckson Tada. Joni and Friends. http://www.joniandfriends.org/.

CBN News. "I Just Had To Know the Lord: Actor Atticus Shaffer Discusses His Faith Journey." Posted May 22, 2018. http://www1.cbn.com/cbnnews/entertainment/2018/may/i-just-had-to-know-the-lord-actor-atticus-shaffer-discusses-his-faith-journey. Accessed June 1, 2018

Block, Mathew. "The Spiritualist Origins of You Don't Have a Soul You are a Soul." Posted January 13, 2014. https://www.firstthings.com/blogs/firstthoughts/2014/01/the-spiritualist-origins-of-you-dont-have-a-soul-you-are-a-soul.

Chapter 5

West, Matthew. Hello My Name Is. *Into the Light*. Sparrow Records. 2012

Danielson, Kristen Bradshaw. "Corrie ten Boom: Forgive Your Enemies."YouTube.www.youtube.com/watch?v=p7x27AQ8gks. Accessed February 11, 2015.

Chapter 6

Holmes and Rahe stress scale. Wikipedia.com. www.wikipedia.org/wiki/Holmes_and_Rahe_stress_scale

Irvinetustin. "(Part 1) Steven Curtis Chapman on Larry King." PostedSeptember13,2008.YouTube.https://www.youtube.com/watch?v=6ySghBeUuNM

Capitol Christian Music Group. "Steven Curtis Chapman Talks About Long Way Home." Posted December 19, 2011. YouTube. www.youtube.com/watch?v=1niJsdkHMjw.

Chapman, Steven Curtis. "Long Way Home". *Re:creation*. Sparrow Records, 2011

The American Colony in Jerusalem. Library of Congress. www.loc.gov/exhibits/americancolony/amcolony-family.html. Accessed April 1, 2014

"AboutJohnWalsh."JohnWalsh.com.http://www.johnwalsh.com/about-john-walsh/.

BGEA staff. "Will There be Animals in Heaven?" Billy Graham Evangelistic Association. https://billygraham.org/answer/will-there-be-animals-in-heaven/. Accessed February 12, 2018.

"ITT,wediscussTölpel."ChristianForums.https://www.christianforums.com/threads/itt-we-discuss-t%C3%B6lpel.7503121/. Accessed February 12, 2018.

"His Name was Tölpel." Posted February 1, 2013. Collies of the Meadow.https://colliesofthemeadow.wordpress.com/2013/02/01/his-name-was-tolpel/.

CBS/AP. "Man Found Alive, Kicking in Body Bag at Mississippi Funeral Home." Posted February 28, 2014. CBS News.com. www.cbsnews.com/news/man-found-alive-kicking-in-body-bag-at-mississippi-funeral-home/.

Hanks, Tom and Wright, Robin. *Forrest Gump*. DVD. Directed by Robert Zemeckis. Paramount Home Video, 2001.

Chapter 7

"Beliefnet's Inspirational Quotes." Beliefnet.com. www.beliefnet.com/quotes/christian/s/st-augustine/god-loves-each-of-us-as-if-there-were-only-one-of.aspx

New York AP. "Tebow: I Don't Know What My Future Holds." PostedJanuary15,2013.SportsIllustrated.https://www.si.com/nfl/2013/01/15/tim-tebow-future-uncertain

Ford, Harrison and Connery, Sean. *Indiana Jones and the Last Crusade*. VHS. Directed by Steven Spielberg. Paramount Home Video, 1996.

Chapter 9

Kübler-Ross, Elisabeth. On Death and Dying: What the Dying Have to Teach Doctors, Nurses, Clergy and Their Own Families. New York: Scribner, 1997.

"Legends about Luther: Lightning." Luther.de. www.luther.de/en/blitz.html.

Seligman, ME. Learned Helplessness. *Annual Review of Medicine*. 1972: 23, (1), 407-412.

Spirit 1053. "Casting Crowns – Praise You in The Storm – Story Behind the Song." Posted on August 15, 2011. You Tube. https://www.youtube.com/watch?v=MNnF7FjZ5po

Casting Crowns. Praise You in This Storm. *Lifesong*. Beach Street/Reunion Records, 2006

Billingsley, Peter, Dillon, Melinda and McGavin, Darren. *A Christmas Story*. DVD. Directed by Bob Clark. Turner Entertainment Co. and Warner Bros. Entertainment Inc., 2006.

Chapter 10

"Albert Einstein Quotes." Brainy Quote. www.brainyquote.com/quotes/albert_einstein_100656

Chapter 11

"Eighteen Martin Luther Quotes that Still Ring True." Posted October31,2017.RelevantMagazine.www.relevantmagazine.com /god/15-martin-luther-quotes-still-ring-true.

"Short Quotes by Martin Luther." Praying the Gospels. www.prayingthegospels.com/martin-luther-church-postils-quotes-2/short-quotes-martin-luther/.

"Quotes:LaLanneisms."JackLaLanne.http://jacklalanne.com/quotes/

Marshall, JL. "Get a Dog and Start Walking." Posted March 15, 2013. *Medscape.* www.medscape.com/viewarticle/780807

"Third Day-I Need a Miracle-Story Behind the Song." 20thecountdownmagazine.www.20thecountdownmagazine.com/ video/third-day-i-need-a-miracle-story-behind-the-song/.

Third Day. I Need a Miracle. *Miracle*. Essential Records, 2012.

Third Day. Cry out to Jesus. *Wherever You Are*. Essential Records. 2005

Leaf, Caroline. Switch On Your Brain: The Key to Peak Happiness, Thinking, and Health. Grand Rapids, MI: Baker Books, 2013.

Casting Crowns. The Voice of Truth. *Casting Crowns*. Beach Street Records, 2004.

Emmons, RA and McCullough, ME. Counting Blessings versus Burdens: an Experimental Investigation of Gratitude and Subjective Well-Being in Daily Life. *Journal of Personality and Social Psychology*. 2003: 84, (2), 377-389.

"Happiness Is A Butterfly, Which When Pursued, Seems Always Just Beyond Your Grasp." Quote Investigator. http://quoteinvestigator.com/2014/04/17/butterfly/.

Chapter 12

Robbins, Tim and Freeman, Morgan. *The Shawshank Redemption*. DVD. Directed by Frank Darabont. Warner Home Video, 1999.

Pringle, Catherine Sager. "Across the Plains in 1844." PBS.org. www.pbs.org/weta/thewest/resources/archives/two/sager1.htm.

Martin, Dewey, Ray, Aldo and Collings, Anne. *Seven Alone*. Directed by Earl Bellamy. Doty-Dayton Production, 1974.

"SagerOrphans."Wikipedia.https://en.wikipedia.org/wiki/Sager_orphans.Accessed November 23, 2016.

Mote, Edward. 1834. My Hope is Built on Nothing Less. The Lutheran Hymnal. #370. Concordia Publishing House. 1941. St. Louis

www.ingramcontent.com/pod-product-compliance
Lightning Source LLC
LaVergne TN
LVHW051543070426
835507LV00021B/2385